STUDIES ON THE CHINESE ECONOMY

General Editors: Peter Nolan, Lecturer in Economics and Politics, University of Cambridge, and Fellow and Director of Studies in Economics, Jesus College, Cambridge, England; and Dong Fureng, Professor, Chinese Academy of Social Sciences, Beijing, China

This series analyses issues in China's current economic development, and sheds light upon that process by examining China's economic history. It contains a wide range of books on the Chinese economy past and present, and includes not only studies written by leading Western authorities, but also translations of the most important works on the Chinese economy produced within China. It intends to make a major contribution towards understanding this immensely important part of the world economy.

Published titles include:

Management Decision-Making in Chinese Enterprises

Yuan Lu
Rothmans Research Fellow
The Judge Institute of Management Studies
University of Cambridge

Foreword by Malcolm Warner

First published in Great Britain 1996 by
MACMILLAN PRESS LTD
Houndmills, Basingstoke, Hampshire RG21 6XS
and London
Companies and representatives
throughout the world

A catalogue record for this book is available
from the British Library.

ISBN 0-333-61948-X

First published in the United States of America 1996 by
ST. MARTIN'S PRESS, INC.,
Scholarly and Reference Division,
175 Fifth Avenue,
New York, N.Y. 10010

ISBN 0-312-15850-5

Library of Congress Cataloging-in-Publication Data
Lu, Yuan.
Management decision-making in Chinese enterprises / Yuan Lu.
p.   cm. — (Studies on the Chinese economy)
Includes bibliographical references and index.
ISBN 0-312-15850-5 (cloth)
1. Industrial management—China.   2. Decision making—China.
I. Title. II. Series.
HD70.C5L82   1996
658.4'03'00951—dc20   95-48387
                                                   CIP

10   9   8   7   6   5   4   3   2   1
05   04   03   02   01   00   99   98   97   96

Printed and bound in Great Britain by
Antony Rowe Ltd, Chippenham, Wiltshire

To Lili and Duncan

Contents

List of Tables

List of Figures

List of Abbreviations

CEMI	China–Europe Management Institute
CLS	Contract Labour System
CPC	Communist Party of China
CRS	Contract Responsibility System
DRS	Director Responsibility System
MEC	Municipal Economic Commission
MPC	Municipal Planning Commission
PRS	Profit Retention System
RLO	Rationalizing Labour Organization
SCRES	State Commission for Restructuring the Economic System
SEC	State Economic Commission
SPC	State Planning Commission

Foreword

Dr Yuan Lu's monograph is one of the few books on Chinese management to combine a Western conceptual framework with empirical data collected on-site. I first met the author over ten years ago in Beijing, when he was initially an MBA student and later Co-Dean of CEMI (the China–Europe Management Institute) and head of the field research on Chinese industrial enterprises being carried out by faculty and groups of students on the MBA programme there. It was all very exciting in those heady days when Western-inspired management ideas were being introduced in China after a lapse of many decades. Yuan Lu worked closely with Professors Max Boisot and John Child at the Institute, and was a key figure in gaining access to local Chinese enterprises and managers in the Beijing area.

The benefit to the faculty and the MBA students involved in this ongoing research was the collective sharing of experiences when carrying out the empirical investigation, both as 'field investigators' for CEMI, and as 'consultants' to the enterprises involved. The firms also benefited from the useful feedback generated at this crucial point in the early and uncertain enterprise reform period.

This book is a result of many years of analysis and reflection by Yuan Lu, first at CEMI and then at Aston University (where he completed his doctorate in management), followed by his current Research Fellowship at the Judge Institute of Management Studies at Cambridge University. It is based on a comprehensive study of Chinese and English-language literature on the subject, as well as an exhaustive empirical field investigation.

The research described in this monograph is one of the most detailed descriptions of managerial decision-making in Chinese state-owned enterprises (SOEs) available. It covers the six firms that CEMI chose to concentrate upon and examines their strategic decisions in areas such as investment, personnel and so on during the critical years of 1985–89, when the economic reforms in China were being introduced.

Following the founding scholars of decision-making theory, Yuan Lu takes a 'strategic' approach and then tries to link activities to decision outcomes. The methodology applied is as advanced as that of any comparable Western-based study. In the eight chapters of the book the author covers in rich detail not only what is generalizable, but also that which is specifically Chinese. He covers the managerial and the political dimensions with great insight, especially as the state enterprises studied were heavily influenced by government policy.

The SOEs' share of industrial output sharply declined from 78 per cent in 1980 to 43 per cent in 1994, but this was largely a result of the growth of the non-state sector. Even so they still employ over a hundred million people, which constitutes an 'iron rice-bowl' for many individuals, although this is now being eroded with the latest wave of reforms. Overmanning is however still rife, with a huge amount of fixed and human capital invested in these enterprises.

Given its concentration in strategic industrial activities, the state enterprise sector in China remains a key lever of the economy (although less than it has been in past years). Many SOEs (well over a third, even using official estimates) make huge losses, therefore reform of such firms is crucial to the completion of the reform process set in train by Deng Xiaoping in the early 1980s. Such reforms are still on-going and may lead if not to 'privatization' then to a form of 'corporatization' with 'Chinese characteristics'.

Yuan Lu has produced one of the best analyses available to the student of Chinese management as to how the reforms were introduced, where they are currently going and where the future evolution of management in SOEs is likely to go. I therefore commend this book to researchers, teachers and students of Chinese management with the fullest confidence that they will learn a great deal concerning the past, present and future of strategic decision-making in such large concerns, and as a consequence will gain valuable insights into both Chinese managerial theory and behaviour. This study, I believe, may in due course be regarded as a model of its kind, and will confidently stand alongside the major studies of Chinese state-owned enterprises carried out by Western management scholars with an interest in this field, such as Child, Granick, Schurmann, Walder and others.

Since China is regarded as the aspirant 'economic superpower' of the next century, it is surely important for those interested in both economics and management studies to gain an insight into the legacy Chinese managers have inherited from the recent past, and how the new generation of managers can learn from the constraints of the past enterprise system to create a new set of benchmarks in order to harness the potent 'Confucian dynamic' set in motion by the Dengist reforms, which have sustained the impressive economic growth rates of the late 1980s and early 1990s.

MALCOLM WARNER

Acknowledgements

I should like to acknowledge the financial support provided by the European Foundation for Management Development and the Rothmans Research Fellowship. I am also indebted to all the managers who gave so willingly of their time to enable me to complete the case studies. I am particularly grateful to Professor John Child, my former supervisor. I should also like to acknowledge the help given by the China–Europe Management Institute, the China Enterprise Management Association and many individuals: David Hickson, Max Boisot, Stewart Clegg, Henry Tosi, Malcolm Warner, Robert Ackroyd, Derek Hugh, Mark Easterby Smith, Peter Nolan, Ginger Chi and David Lake. My thanks also go to Patricia Wilson, who read the manuscript and made some helpful suggestions. Finally, I owe everything to my wife, Lili, and my son, Duncan, for their unfailing encouragement and support.

YUAN LU

Introduction

This book is about Chinese management decision-making during the years 1985 to 1988–89, a period in which the government adopted decentralization as the key to reforming state enterprises. A central objective of this decentralization programme was to delegate decision-making from government agencies to enterprise management. The following chapters examine the effect of decentralization on managerial behaviour, and, more importantly, illustrate the complex relationship between enterprises and their environment. This unique study records and compares industrial changes in six enterprises in Beijing, and provides insights into the decision-making process within these enterprises.

There are three reasons for my choosing this subject. First, the study of decision-making has become one of the most discussed management topics, and scholars have developed various models to conceptualize decision-making processes within organizations. Attention has been drawn to the relationship between the organization and its environment. Theories of organizational decision-making, in fact, are theories of organizational responses to the environments in which organizations operate. However most of this research has been conducted in industrialized countries with market economies. Few empirical studies show how management decisions are taken in China – a country committed to a socialist economy and alien to most Western nations – with respect to the roles of government and managers, and to the political dominance of the Communist Party on society and culture. This book aims to redress this omission by applying Western management theory to Chinese decision-making.

I have tried to answer two questions: (1) 'what factors influence enterprise decision-making?', where my focus has been placed specifically on the relationships between state enterprises, planning authorities and the market; and (2) 'what implications does Chinese management have for the development of modern management theory?'

This research has been constructed around a comparison of similar decisions occurring in each of the six enterprises from 1985 to 1989. It has attempted to identify whether or not similar decisions followed a similar process within each enterprise, and what factors determined the relationship between those decisions and processes. Furthermore it has tried to identify whether or not the decision-making processes in the different organizations were similar when the decisions dealt with similar matters, for instance purchasing or organizational change. All these questions were examined systematically.

Second, I have attempted to examine the progress of and the problems associated with the reform of state enterprises between 1985 and 1989. The strategy of China's economic reform was to increase the autonomy of enterprises by reducing state planning and passing on decision-making power from the planning authorities[1] to enterprise management. As this book seeks to show, this 'evolutionary' approach had the advantage of maintaining state control and preventing large-scale chaos. Nevertheless there were challenges, and as the traditional centrally planned economy moved towards a market one, resistance came from the existing planning system. Therefore one can ask to what extent the reform policy gave rise to real change in the nature of the managerial processes within enterprises.

Third, I was fortunate in gaining access to the six enterprises in order to study them. From 1985–86 I participated in an MBA programme at the China–Europe Management Institute (CEMI), where I established contact with the six enterprises. In 1988–89 I was appointed as co-dean of CEMI to supervise MBA students carrying out projects in these enterprises. This gave me the opportunity to continue my study and compare the changes in management decision-making processes. Many managers eventually became good friends, sparing their time for lengthy interviews and allowing me access to important documents.

THEORETICAL PERSPECTIVES AND RESEARCH DESIGN

In my research I have attempted to identify a discrepancy between the theory of the reform policy and its practical application to enterprise management through an investigation of decision-making processes. Making decisions is without doubt one of the most important functions of management. Decisions taken by managers will determine the future of their organizations, and their decisions are usually labelled as 'strategic' or 'top' decisions. Simon (1976) referred to 'decision-making' as the synonym for management. Decision-making refers to a set of activities leading to implementation. A decision could concern economic transactions, such as purchasing and pricing. It could be triggered by the managers desire to change the organization so as to fit the organizational structure to the competitive environment. In general, organizational decision-making processes are regarded as important, complex and collective. They are important because the outcome of decisions has a bearing upon the performance of the organization and may determine its survival. They are complex because managers have to take risks and face uncertainties in the competitive environment. They are collective, since many actors – individuals or groups from internal departments and those from outside the organization – may participate in the decision-making process.

This research followed Pettigrew and his colleagues' (Pettigrew, 1985a, 1988, 1989) suggestion that managerial behaviour can be understood through the study of *decision contents* (kinds), *decision processes* and *decision contexts*. Contents in this sense means the issues that the decision is attempting to solve. The five main issues in organizational decision-making are as follows:

1. The purchase of inputs – how enterprises decide to select and procure supplies such as raw materials.
2. Product pricing – how enterprise managers determine the price of their goods.
3. Recruitment – the selection of new employees and head-hunting as result of job mobilization.
4. Organizational change – rearrangement of the organization's structure and changing its size.
5. Product innovation and/or investment in production processes – strategic activities relating to new product development and production expansion through investing in a new site.

These five kinds of decision were compared twice in the six enterprises, in 1985 and 1988–89; that is, 60 decisions in all were studied.

The decision-making process is mainly concerned with activities leading to a decision outcome (Hickson *et al.*, 1986; Pettigrew, 1973; Mintzberg *et al.*, 1976), and it consists of some basic components in a time framework that starts with the first proposal and finishes when the decision is approved. Between start and finish the activities can be grouped into the proposal itself, its design, assessment and approval. Each of these activities is undertaken by one or more actors. The actors may be internal or external, and their involvement indicates the extent of their power at the organizational level, as well as their different interests.

The decision-making context refers to the operational settings embedded in the environment in which the enterprise operates. This research focuses on three operational settings. The first is internal to the

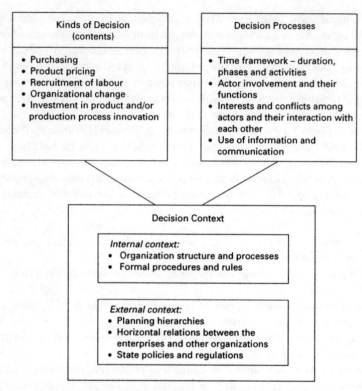

Sources: Summarized from Hickson *et al.* (1986), Yuan Lu (1991), Mintzberg *et al.* (1976) and Pettigrew (1985a, 1989).

Figure 1.1   The decision-making model

enterprise: its organizational structure, functions and procedures, or the internal rules dealing with decision-making activities. The second is the state planning regime, which plays a most important role in state enterprises. Management decision-making in China is set in a web of complex relations with various authorities. These networks are embedded in the planning hierarchy, through which state intervention is exerted via ownership control and regulations, plus direct interference in management decision-making. The third is concerned with links between the enterprise and other organizations to facilitate transactions and resource mobilization. The decision-making model proposed in this research is exhibited in Figure 1.1.

Following Pettigrew's (1989) notion, this research involves consideration of not only the content of the decision and the analytical process, but also the context in which the decision occurs. The content of the decision is the 'what' of the issues being decided upon. The 'how' of decision-making can be understood by examining the process, and the 'why' from analysis of the context. The central theme of this model is to explore linkages among the three aspects and their changes during the time of the study.

The research methodology incorporated semi-structured interviews with the managers involved in the decisions identified. Each interviewee also responded to a questionnaire (see Appendix), which examined the process with regard to duration, actor involvement, decision levels, interaction between actors and information communication procedures. A survey was conducted whenever access to documents was permitted. Project assignments carried out by CEMI on management in the six enterprises and MBA students' reports were complementary sources of data.

This book has eight chapters. Chapter 1 provides a brief overview of China's experience of industrialization from 1949 to 1984. Emphasis is given to an analysis of industrial decision-making and the evolutionary progress of decentralization. Chapter 2 examines the reform programme in urban industries after 1984, when the state eventually adopted a decentralization programme as the key to reforming state enterprises. This chapter also provides an outline of industrial enterprises in Beijing and provides profiles of the six enterprises selected for this research. Chapter 3 studies changes in purchasing decisions, which were coordinated by state plans in 1985 and moved towards the market mechanism from 1988 onwards. Chapter 4 provides a detailed examination of price reform and how the state administrative mechanism, as a contradictory force to market demand, constrained price determination in the enterprises. Chapter 5 analyses decisions about labour recruitment, which had been delegated to the enterprises. Chapter 6 concerns organizational change and evaluates the extent to which decision-making power was transferred from the Communist Party secretary to the directors in 1985 and 1988. Chapter 7 looks at investment decisions with regard to product and/or production innovation, where the government still imposed constraints in 1988–89. Chapter 8 summarizes the research findings, provides an update on the reforms (1993) and concludes the study.

1 Industrial Governance and Enterprise Management in China 1949–84

1.1 STATE SOCIALISM IN CHINA: INSTITUTIONAL STRUCTURE AND INDUSTRIAL GOVERNANCE

China turned to state socialism after 1949 when the Communist Party took power.[1] In choosing socialism as a development strategy the Chinese government was following the central ideological tenet of socialism. This emphasized collective ownership and identity, in which the state and the Party claimed to represent the interests of the working class as a general collective, and therefore that the hierarchical control of organizations was legitimate. Instead of being motivated by profit, the people were to be motivated by moral and political rewards, and individuals were to render an adequate contribution to the collective effort (Bate and Child, 1987). These ideological principles were applied through a centrally planned economy, in which resource allocation and economic activities were coordinated by state planners (Andors, 1977; Lee, 1987; Schurmann, 1966).

During the early 1950s China established economic institutions and industrial governance that had been learnt from the former Soviet Union. Prior to 1978, when the economic reform started, the Chinese economic system had the following characteristics.[2] First, as state socialism required state ownership, the most important industrial enterprises were owned by the state. This monopoly was realized during the period 1956–58, when the government launched what is known as the 'Socialist Transformation' and systematically eliminated private ownership through nationalization and collectivization (Andors, 1977; Riskin, 1987). As Table 1.1 shows, the proportion of industrial output contributed by the state and collectively owned sectors increased rapidly in 1956, while that of private firms reduced to almost zero. State enterprises[3] thus became the backbone of China's industry.

Second, an institutional framework for central planning[4] was established, with the State Council at the top and under it several state commissions. The two most important commissions with regard to

6

Table 1.1   Proportion of the contribution of different ownership sectors to total industrial output values, 1949–84 (per cent)

Year	State owned	Collectively owned	Privately owned	Other
1949	26.25	0.50	22.97	50.28
1953	43.04	3.87	19.26	33.83
1957	53.77	19.03	0.83	26.37
1958	89.17	10.83	–	–
			–	–
1960	90.60	9.40	–	–
1965	90.07	9.93	–	–
1969	88.71	11.29	–	–
1970	87.61	12.39	–	–
1976	78.33	21.67	–	–
1978	77.63	22.37	–	–
1980	75.97	23.54	0.02	0.48
1984	69.09	29.71	0.19	1.01

* The 'Other' figures for 1949–57 refer to state and private joint-ownership enterprises. Industry in this category refers to industrial enterprises with joint state and collective ownership, shareholding companies, foreign-owned industrial enterprises (that is, sole investment, joint equity ventures and cooperative ventures), and industrial enterprises invested in by overseas Chinese from Hong Kong, Macao, Taiwan and other places.

Source: *China Statistical Yearbook 1992*, p. 408.

economic administration were the State Planning Commission (SPC), established in 1952 and responsible for long-term plans, and the State Economic Commission (SEC), established in 1956 and in charge of annual operational plans. In 1956 the General Bureau for the Supply of Raw Materials was established to handle the allocation of resources and materials. In the same year the State Technology Commission was created to plan long-term technical development.

Below the SPC and SEC there were central functional agencies and industrial ministries. The former consisted of ministries and bureaux acting as regulatory authorities in charge of certain areas, such as finance, labour and personnel, taxation, audits and prices. Industrial ministries dealt with product categories, such as coal, chemicals, machinery, shipbuilding and textiles, and directly administered some industrial enterprises. From 1953 to 1957, for instance, the number of enterprises directly administered by the central ministries increased from 2800 to 9300. Within industrial ministries, there were bureaux in charge of more detailed products. These institutions assigned state plans to enterprises and coordinated most of their transaction activities, for instance the allocation of products and materials. In 1953, 115 industrial products and 227 raw materials were subject to state planning. By the end of 1957 these figures had increased to 290 and 532 respectively (Department of Institutional and Legal Reform of the SPC, 1988). Prior to 1978 almost 100 per cent of industrial products and more than 90 per cent of agricultural goods were allocated according to state plans.[5]

Third, as well as the control exerted by central government agencies, local government participated actively in the economic administration of enterprises (cf. Li Peilin *et al.*, 1992; Zhong Chengxun, 1993). The structure of local government usually corresponded to that of the central government and embraced the local planning and economic commissions and industrial and functional bureaux. Their functions and administrative responsibilities were similar to those of the ministries, and the local bureaux reported to the central ministries. Most medium-sized and small firms were directly controlled by local government.[6]

Fourth, with state socialism, the Communist Party played a dominant role in industrial management and penetrated every aspect of life. During the 1950s, Party members weakened the position of professional managers in decision-making and established their own exclusive leadership in enterprises.[7] 'Politics in command' became the main theme of Chinese management from the late 1950s onwards. The Communist Party organization, while independent from the administrative system, was attached to the organizational structure. Supreme power lay with the Party's Central Committee, under which were ministerial, provincial and municipal Party committees. Below the municipal level, each bureau had a Party committee that was in charge of Party organizations within enterprises: either a Party committee or a Party general branch – depending on the size of the enterprise – headed by the Party secretary. Below that were party branches in workshops and party groups consisting of individual Party members. The Party issued directives and commands, supervised individual Party members and other non-Party staff, determined personnel issues such as promotion and demotion, and provided political education programmes.

As the planning authorities provided detailed specifications of the value of all products, enterprise management was thus confined to the operational task of following the instructions and commands issued as a result of state plans. The reinforcement provided by state planners was the main factor that kept enterprises running along a certain track, and they carried out their production and distribution activities like cogs in a large wheel. Thus the role of management was likely to focus on reconciling conflicts between the planning authorities, the Party, the workforce and other external units, such as suppliers and sellers (cf. Campbell, 1966).

The coordinating mechanisms in the socialist economy relied upon bureaucratic procedures hierarchically structured by state planning. In China the market was artificially depressed by the intervention of state planning and the Party (cf. Berger, 1986). This caused a number of problems. Ma Hong (1979) has pointed out four crucial drawbacks of the central planning system in China. First, as it was impossible to include all commodities in state plans, a large number of products were beyond state control. However, because enterprises arranged their production according to state plans, they had little incentive to produce non-plan commodities. This led to shortages, a common occurrence in socialist economies (cf. Kornai, 1980), and most commodities were unavailable in the market. Second, economic coordination was conducted by administrative command, rather than by transactions between enterprises and their suppliers and/or distributors. Both industrial ministries and local government administered enterprises according to their own interests. Their intervention made economic coordination difficult, and as a consequence the planning and control processes became political and bureaucratic. Third, as a result of state control over every aspect of economic activity, managers had no need to improve their performance, relying instead on the state to allocate resources and production tasks. Fourth, there was a lack of incentives and penalties for enterprise managers and workers. Consequently resources were wasted, and poor performance was inevitable (Ma Hong, 1979).[8]

In addition to the problems caused by state centralization, the Party's dominance in decision-making burdened enterprises with political tasks. Parallel to administrative hierarchies implementing central plans, the Party mechanism coexisted within institutions and organizations to supervise and control activities in accordance with political principles. Political loyalty was the most important criterion for job promotion, which led to the 'political management' style described by Kerr and his colleagues (1960). Hence the organizational structure in China was complicated, and performance assessment was likely to involve the central planning system, the Party organization and the production-technical system (Bate and Child, 1987; Kerr, 1983; Spulber, 1979).

1.2 ATTEMPTS TO IMPROVE PERFORMANCE IN STATE ENTERPRISES THROUGH DECENTRALIZATION IN THE PRE-REFORM PERIOD UP TO 1979

The problems brought about by China's rigid centrally planned economy were recognized as early as the 1950s. In 1958 the central government made its first attempt to solve these problems by decentralizing decision-making and handing it over to local governments. This started with the introduction of a set of policies expanding the scope of businesses, granting profit retention to enterprises, relaxing financial control over enterprise activities and passing on responsibility for investment to local planners. By the end of 1958 more than 8000 state enterprises had been delegated to local governments, and the central ministries only controlled around 1000 large firms. The types of material subject to state planning were reduced from more than 500 to 130. But decentralization soon resulted in economic chaos because local governments wasted resources, and therefore recentralization was reimposed by the central government.[9]

By 1963 industrial management was highly centralized by the state, and 10 000 state enterprises were directly administered by ministries. The state commissions and ministries not only controlled most industrial production, but also governed investment, raw material allocation, product distribution, prices, wages/salaries, number of employees, finances and disposal of assets. Managers protested about such strict centralization, and so in the late 1960s another decentralization scheme was attempted. The administration of small enterprises was handed back to local governments. In 1967 local governments were also allowed to retain enterprise depreciation funds. In 1970 the central government decided to give local authorities more autonomy in managing enterprises. More than 2000 firms, including some large corporations such as the Daqing Oil Field and the Changchun Automobile Factory, became the responsibility of the local authorities. However these measures failed to improve performance and caused problems with economic control – similar to the earlier attempt. In 1975 the central government decided to 'remedy the enterprises' (*qiye zhengdun*), which in effect was yet another return to centralization (Zhu Jiaming and Lu Zheng, 1984; Wu Jinglian, 1992). These experiences were a recurring cycle in China's policy towards industrial decision-making: Centralization leads to rigidity, rigidity leads to complaints, complaints lead to decentralization, decentralization leads to disorder and disorder leads back to centralization (*yizhua jiusi, yisi jiujiao, yijiao jiufang, yifang jiuluan, yiluan jiuzhua*).

Critics of the two decentralization attempts called attention to the level at which decision-making occurred. It was argued that decision-making should have been delegated to enterprises rather than local governments. The nature of decentralization programmes before 1978, Chinese economists argued, was actually a division of power between central and local government, and it was a kind of 'administrative decentralization' (Liu Guoguang, 1988; Wu Jinglian, 1992), which was mostly based on the theme proposed by Mao in the 'Ten Great Relationships', put forward in 1956. His comments on the relationship between central and local government, and among production units and individuals, became the principle of decentralization (Wu Jinglian, 1992; Zhou Shulian, 1992). Decentralization prior to 1978 was centred around the relationship between the central government and the local authorities and failed to give enterprises decision-making powers. As a result, enterprises operated according to government instructions, either central or local, ignoring customers and the market.

Furthermore, these decentralization programmes were implemented through a political process that became a unique feature of economic administration in China. As Wu Jinglian (1992) has pointed out, the anti-rightist (*fan you*) movement in 1957 and China's deteriorating relationship with the former Soviet Union in the late 1950s meant that any proposal for material incentives and enterprise autonomy risked being criticized as 'revisionist'. In such a political context, the concepts of enterprise decision-making autonomy and the market economy were taboo. Any reform programme had to be disguised by politically acceptable rhetoric. For example decentralization in the 1970s was propagated by political slogans such as 'decentralization is a revolution', and 'more decentralization, more revolution'.[10] As a result the decentralization programmes were implemented without adequate theoretical preparation.

1.3 CHINESE CULTURE AND ITS INFLUENCE ON MANAGEMENT

Chinese culture and society stretch back more than five thousand years. There is a unique cultural heritage of philosophy, science and technology, societal structures and a traditional administrative bureaucracy. No study of management can overlook this cultural legacy. Four key concepts of Chinese culture have been identified.

First, in China there is a traditional respect for age, hierarchy and authority, that originates from the Confucian concept of *li* (rite, propriety), which played an important role in maintaining a person's social position. *Li* helped to sustain the traditional bureaucracy that typified the vertical relationship between emperor, officials and ordinary people. The centralization of decision-making was acceptable in such a cultural context (Lockett, 1988; Yuan Lu, 1988; Pye, 1985; Wei Zhengtong, 1988; Zi Zhongyun, 1987).

Second, Chinese view the family as the essential social unit and there is a strong tendency to promote the collective or the group (Lockett, 1988; Wei Zhengtong, 1988). Within the family or group, members must maintain harmonious relationships. Thus the family or clan norms are adopted as the formal code of conduct, and members are bound to these standards.[11]

Third, the concept of 'face' (*mianzi*) is seen as an important feature. As Hu (1944, p. 45) noted, the concept of *mianzi* related to 'a reputation achieved through getting on in life through success and ostentation'. Hwang (1983) has argued that in a static society, such as traditional China, where the major social resources were controlled by a few allocators distributing resources in accordance with their personal preferences, the game of *mianzi* is played for the purpose of strengthening relationships with others. Furthermore *mianzi* also serves to enhance harmony within the family or group, so that only the positive is expressed publicly and any conflicts remain private.

Fourth is the value of personal relations (*guanxi*). This constitutes an interpersonal network, where social exchanges are shared or reciprocated (Hwang, 1983). According to Hwang's model, *guanxi* refers to relationships outside an individual's immediate family. Persons with *guanxi* usually share a common birthplace, lineage, surname or experience, such as attending the same school, working together or belonging to the same organization (Jacobs, 1979). A comparative study of decision-making in China and Britain has revealed that Chinese managers use their personal *guanxi* more widely to exchange information, negotiate with planning authorities and accelerate decision-making processes than managers from British firms (Lu and Heard, 1995).

In modern China these traditional concepts are still very significant. In a survey of people in 324 cities in 1988, attributes such as honesty, patriotism and respect for parents came top of the list of social values. As for national characteristics, people were seen as diligent, thrifty, practical, conservative and obedient (*Beijing Review*, no. 5, 1988). Laaksonen (1988) noted that in modern China, business and industrial enterprises were perceived as an extension of the family system. Thus '[s]ubordinates were generally expected to be unquestioningly loyal,

Table 1.2   Chinese traditional culture, the ideologies of state socialism and their implications for enterprise management

Ideological tenets of state socialism	Chinese traditional culture	Implication for management practice
Centralized planning system and state monopolized control	Respect for authorities	Centralization in decision-making; vertical communication with the authorities
Collective leadership; political incentives and disciplines	Collectivism, group-oriented behaviour and harmonious relations between individuals	Viewing an enterprise as a family-like multiple functional unit, including economic, political and social obligations
Negotiated order along the hierarchy	Importance of personal relations and family kinship	The dynamics of power between boss and employee; bargaining relations between individuals
Presenting one's good side	Concept of *mianzi*	Presenting one's good side; informal behaviour and communication other than formal regulations and procedures

Sources: Summarized from Hwang (1983), Lockett (1988), Yuan Lu (1988), Ma Quanshan (1989), Shenkar and Ronan (1987), Schurmann (1966) and Zi Zhongyun (1987).

obedient, and subservient in executing the orders and instructions issued by their superiors' (ibid., p. 95). This argument is consistent with Shenkar and Ronan's (1987) finding that mainland Chinese managers hold a deep belief in collectivism in organizations, viewing challenges as collective endeavours rather than meeting individual goals. They also view work as more important than leisure and as contributing to their family welfare rather than competing with it. Finally, they consider that collectivity is more important than individualism. Redding and Ng (1982) have found that the concept of *mianzi* still plays an important role in social relationships and organizational behaviour.

These key concepts of Chinese culture are quite compatible with socialist ideology, as indicated in Table 1.2. The imperial monopoly of China's political and economic life is consistent with socialist principles of state ownership, central planning processes and the party's dominant position. The Chinese preference for family-based boundaries and group-oriented collectivity is also compatible with socialist ideologies that emphasize collectivism and moral incentives.

As Table 1.2 indicates, socialist ideological principles and culture can jointly affect management practice. Yet certain aspects of Chinese culture could cause problems under a centrally planned economy. For example the Chinese respect for authority could be interpreted as a large 'power distance' (cf. Hofstede, 1980). Organizational decision-making in such a context is perceived to favour centralization, which would make it difficult to resolve problems in a centrally planned economy since it inhibits any challenge to the planning authorities (Lockett, 1988; Yuan Lu, 1988). With this large power distance, plus the concept of *mianzi*, information communication could be limited within the vertical hierarchy, and horizontal communications could be impeded (cf. Child, 1994).

Since collectivism is compatible with China's family and group orientation, it is possible to view an enterprise as an extended family. Consequently enterprise management is required to undertake multiple functions that combine economic, political and social obligations (Li Peilin *et al.*, 1992). This phenomenon is what Walder (1989) calls the 'four facts of life.' The first is that the enterprise is a political coalition, in which management requires the support of other enterprise officials, particularly the Party secretary. The second is that the enterprise is a social–political community, with management being judged on social criteria by both the Party and the trade unions. The third is the continued importance of vertical relationships with the government bureaucracy, which could influence management's ability to achieve prosperity for its enterprise. The fourth is the continuing importance of non-market exchange relationships, particularly in securing scarce supplies and sales credit.

1.4   START OF THE ECONOMIC REFORM AND THE PILOT PROGRAMME OF 1979–83: DECENTRALIZATION IN SELECTED REGIONS

On 22 December 1978 at the Third Plenum of the 11th Central Committee, the Communist Party officially announced its plan for economic reform. Emphasis was placed on continuing the ambitious modernization plans proposed by Mao and Zhou Enlai in the early 1970s.[12] The reform began in the rural areas, but from 1979 the focus gradually moved to industrial enterprises and some pilot programmes were initiated in selected regions. Although the essence of these programmes was decentralization, they attracted attention because decision-making power was transferred from the planning authorities to enterprises.

From 5–28 April 1979 the Party Central Committee held a conference, at which it was decided to implement a plan of 'readjustment, reform, remedy and improvement' (*tiaozheng, gaige, zhengdun, tigao*) to correct the political and economic chaos caused by the Cultural Revolution. On 25 May 1979 six central government agencies (the SEC, the Finance Ministry, the Foreign Trade Ministry, the People's Bank of China, the General Bureau for the Supply of Raw Material and the General Bureau of Labour) issued a document entitled 'On key points at the conference concerning the enterprise management reform experiment' (*guanyu qiye guanli gaige shidian zuotan hui de jiyao*). This initiated a pilot programme of reform in eight state enterprises in Beijing, Tianjin and Shanghai.

On 13 July 1979 the State Council issued its first five policy documents, the most important of which concerned the expansion of enterprise autonomy by:

- allowing enterprises to plan their production on condition they fulfilled the state plans;
- introducing a profit-retention system, linking rewards to employees to realized profits;
- gradually increasing the rate of depreciation and allowing enterprises to use their depreciation funds for innovation;
- implementing a fixed-assets-payment system, permitting enterprises to dispose of their surplus assets;
- using bank loans for the supply of current assets;
- encouraging new product development;
- encouraging enterprises to apply for export status and allowing them to retain part of their foreign currency earnings;
- allowing enterprises to recruit workers and make their own incentive policies;
- allowing enterprises to design their own organizational structure and implement organizational change according to task requirements.

Local governments also organized various pilot programmes. By the end of June 1980 more than 6000 state enterprises had been selected to test different decentralization schemes. On 2 September 1980 the State Council advanced the decentralization programme by publishing the SEC document: 'Report on experiments of expansion of enterprise autonomy and suggestions for the future' (*guanyu kuoda qiye zizhuquan shidian gongzuo qingkuang he jinhou yijian de baogao*) whereby decision-making power in aspects of pricing, profit sharing and the use of capital were passed from the government to enterprise management.

On 20 May 1981 ten government agencies – including the State Council's Finance and Economic System Reform Office, the SPC, the SEC, the Ministries of Finance, Commerce, Labour and Foreign Trade, the General Bureau for the Supply of Raw Materials and the People's Bank of China – jointly issued a detailed policy, referred to as the '60 points' (*liushi tiao*). This document delegated a further 12 decision-making powers to enterprises with regard to production planning, profit retention, use of capital, sale of products, product development, exports and the retention of foreign currency earnings, pricing policy, taxation, bank credit and loans, organizational design, personnel and labour management, the reduction of social obligations and democratic management approaches. What emerged from these measures became known as the industrial economic responsibility system (*gongye jingji zeren zhi*).

The central theme of this system was clarification of the responsibilities of the state, the enterprises and individuals, to be accomplished by incentives aimed at motivating them. During 1982 and 1983 the reform of state enterprises concentrated on decentralization measures, mainly continuing the earlier decentralization programmes. But there were some differences in the level and scope of the reforms (Wu Jinglian, 1992). The first was that decentralization was not only at the local government level, but was extended to include enterprise management. The second was the introduction of non-state sectors in agriculture and foreign trade in response to the open-door policy.

The experiment with decentralization seemed to progress satisfactorily. According to a report from Sichuan Province, of 100 pilot enterprises, 84 increased their output values by 14.9 per cent from 1978 to 1979 while their profits increased by 33 per cent (Ren Tao et al., 1980). By the end of 1980 the total output of 5777 pilot enterprises participating in the decentralization experiment in 28 provinces and municipalities had increased by 6.8 per cent, compared with that in 1979, while profit increased by 11.8 per cent (Zhu Jiaming and Lu Zheng, 1984). On the other hand, there emerged some problems that produced unintended results (Lin Zili, 1980; Wu Jinglian, 1992). The biggest difficulty was that enterprises were constrained by state planning in the supply and distribution network because the most important raw materials were subject to planning quotas. The market remained in a primitive state, coordinating transactions between enterprises. For instance prices were strictly controlled by the government and distribution networks were monopolized by ministries and bureaux. Therefore in reality enterprises were unable to buy inputs or sell their output without the permission of the planning authorities. Moreover, even decisions concerning internal issues such as labour management and organization design were limited by government bureaux agencies. In order to transform state enterprises into units coordinated according to market demands, the decentralization programme was moved into the second stage, in which the reform of the whole planning system and more radical delegation were adopted, as will be discussed in the next chapter.

2 Economic Reform: Decentralization 1984–88

2.1 DECENTRALIZATION AND REFORM IN URBAN AREAS AFTER 1984

Between 1984 and 1988 there were dramatic changes in China's reform policies. First, enterprises became the focus of the reform and decentralization was formally adopted as *the* programme on a national scale. On 10 May 1984 the State Council published one of its most important policies endorsing decentralization: 'Temporary regulations on further expansion of autonomy in large and medium-sized state enterprises' (*guanyu jinyibu kuoda guoying gongye qiye zizuquan de zhanxing guiding*), granting enterprises autonomy in 10 areas. These were production planning, product sales, pricing, supplies, the use of capital retained from profits, disposal of unnecessary assets, management of labour and personnel, organizational design, rewards and salary/wage setting and the formation of industrial groups among enterprises. This policy was the first to legislate the scope of enterprise management.

Closely associated with the decentralization programme was a reform programme in urban areas. In May 1984 the SCRES (State Commission for Restructuring the Economic System) circulated 'Key points of the Working Conference on an Experiment of Economic Institutional Reform in Urban Cities' (*guanyu chengshi jingji tizhi gaige shidian gongzuo zuotan hui de jiyao*). The purpose of the urban reform, as proposed in the general programme in December 1979,[1] was to simplify government administrative systems and create a suitable context in which to ensure enterprise autonomy through the decentralization programme.

Second, these policies were driven by a set of concepts developed from Deng Xiaoping's ideology to modernize China through a mixed economy consisting of state planning and market forces. For Deng, the driving force behind society's development was not the class struggle, but the forces of production:

> We have done mainly two things: we have set wrong things right, and we have launched comprehensive reform. For many years, we

suffered badly from one major error: we still take class struggle as the key link. And we neglected the development of the productive forces (Deng Xiaoping, 1985; quoted in Clarke, 1986, p. 120).

This effort of 'setting wrong things right' was seen in the attempt to build up two dominant perspectives. One was 'a socialist commercial economy' (*shehui zhuyi shangpin jingji*), endorsing the view that state planning must dominate economic activity and that strategic industries should remain under public ownership, while the market plays a complementary role in assisting state control.[2] The other was 'primary socialism' (*chuji shehui zhuyi*), based on the premise that socialism in China was still at a preliminary stage where the market was a necessary apparatus to coordinate enterprise operations. This was the first time that the concept of the market was accepted in official ideology. These two theories were combined into a formula: 'The state guides the market, the market directs enterprises' (Zhao Ziyang, 1987, 1988). These concepts differed from Maoism in many aspects, and they shaped the reform policies after 1984, not only to increase enterprise autonomy, but also to change economic institutions, including the state planning system and Party organizations. Table 2.1 compares the key concepts concerning industrial management.

The decentralization programme after 1984 focused on two schemes. The first was to separate the government from enterprise operations (*zhengqi fenkai*). This aimed to keep state ownership separate from management control and to turn state enterprises into economic units pursuing profitability rather than production units following state commands. The second was to remove the Party from direct enterprise management (*dangzheng fenkai*), with the director as the main authority in management decision-making and the Party in a supporting role.

A number of policies were issued after May 1984 to advance the decentralization programme. In February 1985 the State Council approved a policy proposal by the SEC, the Ministry of Finance and the People's Bank of China. This was 'Temporary regulations regarding respective policy issues concerning the promotion of technological innovation in state enterprises' (*guanyu tuijin guoying qiye jishu jinbu ruogan zhengce de zhanxing guiding*), and it encouraged renovation and innovation through the profit retention system. In July the State Council raised its threshold regarding bonus taxes and published its new regulations on wages and bonuses, giving more powers to enterprises. In September, the State Council granted a policy to activate large and medium-sized enterprises, with emphasis on decision-making

Table 2.1   Differences of concepts concerning enterprise management
before and during the reform

Concept	Before the reform	During the reform (mainly from 1984)
1. Ownership	Monopoly of state ownership in most economic sectors	Mix of multiple ownership consisting of state and private
2. Social development driving force	Class struggle	Productive force, mainly technology
3. Central task of the Party and nation	Continuous revolution	Economic construction and the 'four modernizations'
4. Role of the Party in enterprises	Unified leadership in all issues	Supporting, monitoring and supervising managers
5. Role of the state in economic administration	Overcentralized planning and control over economic activities	Mix of state plans and market
6. Role of the market	Chaos and anarchy as a capitalist economy, opposite to socialism	A complementary mechanism to coordinate enterprise operations
7. Definition of an enterprise	Basic political organization and an operational unit of the central planning system	Economic agent with autonomy in operations and business activities
8. Enterprise performance	Following instructions from the state, the Party and central plans	Achievement of profitability, plus objectives of public interest and state plans
9. Relationship between enterprises and government	Government as both the administrative and regulatory authority over enterprises	Government as a regulatory authority and supervisor of enterprises
10. Body of management decision-making	The Party Committee	Enterprise directors
11. Criteria of personnel promotion	Political loyalty	Professional knowledge, managerial competence, political loyalty, age and health
12. Incentive/reward policies	Political motivation and non-material incentives; egalitarian allocation of wages	Material incentives linked to the individual performance

Sources: Summarized from Barnowe (1990), Hussain (1990), Lee (1986), Liu Guoguang (1988), Liu Yaojin (1989), Maxwell and McFarlane (1984).

autonomy, improving employee qualifications and quality management, and reducing state plans.

At the same time the government realized that constraints on enterprise decision-making were resulting from the imperfect market. Therefore the reform should aim to create a proper institutional environment, in which traditional planning systems must be changed. In the Seventh Five-Year Plan the government announced reform strategies for broader areas, including pricing, taxation, monetary supply, financing and banking (Zhao Ziyang, 1986). In March 1986 the State Council published a policy to promote collaboration between firms. In July a set of four related regulations concerning labour management were issued, giving enterprise managers the power to determine recruitment, contractual labour and dismissal of unqualified and unsatisfactory workers. In September the Party's Central Committee and the State Council jointly published three policies aimed at regulating relations among the directors, the Party and the Workers' Congress in state enterprises. At that time, decision-making powers were transferred from Party secretaries to directors. In November, the Central Committee and the State Council jointly circulated a regulation stressing that directors were to be the main authorities in enterprise decision-making. In December the Enterprise Bankrupt Law was passed at the 18th Plenum of the Sixth National People's Congress. In the same month the State Council published a policy aimed at ensuring that enterprise autonomy would not be handicapped by government agencies.[3]

Political uncertainty clouded the start of 1987. A campaign to denounce 'Anti-capitalist bourgeoism' (*fandui zichan jieji ziyouhua*) was launched to create obstacles to the reforms. Hu Yaobang, the Central Party Committee secretary who held a liberal view regarding political reform, was forced to resign. This political instability affected the decentralization programme, and the issue of removing the Party from management was questioned as to whether or not it meant eliminating Party leadership in enterprise management. But in reality it was difficult, after three years of practice, to reverse the decentralization programme. Therefore 1987 saw numerous policies emphasizing the continuity of decentralization. Moreover reform programmes were started in national economic institutions, such as monetary mechanisms, finance, infrastructure and technology innovation. Factor markets such as stock and securities, labour and technology were established to mobilize labour and other resources. Some important policies were launched. These included Zhao Ziyang's government report in March, calling for an expansion of the reforms in various institutional spheres; the State

Council's policy in April, granting large firms the power to make plans independently of the ministries; and the State Council's decision to implement the director responsibility system (DRS) on a large scale.[4] In October the 13th National Congress confirmed the reforms and called for market development and greater separation of the Party from enterprise management. All these advanced the decentralization programme. By the end of 1987, more than 70 per cent of state enterprises, of which there were 44 000, had adopted the DRS (Wu Zhenkun and Chen Wentong, 1993). In 1988 all state enterprises were required to implement the DRS.

During the early stages of the reform there were some experiments with profit contract systems, the first of which was in Guangdong Province in 1978. In 1981 the contract system was introduced in a small group of firms, such as Shougang. From 1987 system was given a higher profile. In April 1987 the SEC, on behalf of the State Council, organized a working conference, in which it advocated implementation of the enterprise contract business responsibility system or the contract responsibility system (CRS) for short. An enterprise in the CRS was held to a profit contract for a fixed term. By the end of July 1987, 56.8 per cent of large and medium-sized firms had signed a profit contract. In February 1988 the government decided to implement the CRS in most enterprises[5] and the State Council announced a regulation regarding contract systems. The CRS was seen as the ultimate measure to ensure decentralization, as the relationship between the government and enterprises was legislated through contract compliance rather than planning quotas or other administrative measures.

Reform of the state planning systems was also in progress. In May 1987 the State Council announced a programme to establish 120 raw material exchange centres as a market beyond the planning quotas. By 1987 the SPC had reduced its planning quotas on strategic industrial products from 120 categories in 1979 to about 60, and raw materials subject to state distribution had been reduced in number from 256 to 26. Then the SEC was dissolved. Some of its functions (concerning technological innovation and operation plans) were taken over by the SPC, the rest by the SCRES. In July 1988 local governments were given greater power to make investment decisions, but the SPC retained control of key industrial sectors and large construction projects. In August the Enterprise Law came into effect, which legislated that state enterprises were to be economic units responsible for profitability.

However, as the economic institutions were transferred from central planning to a mixed economy, the environment became turbulent and unstable. After 1985, inflation started to threaten the price reforms when the government introduced a dual-price system. This applied to three categories of prices: state-set, state-guided (or floating) and free market (for details, see Chapter 4). Because state-set prices were much lower than the market ones and most of the products that were subject to state price control were in short supply, enterprises could earn extra profits by shifting their products from state planning to the market. Thus the price of raw materials and other commodities shot up. In the summer of 1988 panic buying occurred in major municipalities and cities, triggered by a fear of inflation. This shocked those at the top, and therefore the Politburo of the Central Party Committee decided to halt the price reform in favour of state control over pricing policies. In September the Central Party Committee, in order to remedy the economic situation, decided to resume control of most economic activities.

In 1989 the reforms were put on hold and most economic measures concerning decentralization were almost reversed. The political upheavals from April to June in Beijing caused the fall of Zhao Ziyang, who had favoured the market economy. The political struggle at the top undermined the economic reforms, and politics dominated economic development. The government continued to 'remedy and adjust' (*zhili zhengdun*) both enterprise management and the economic environment through the recentralization of economic decision-making. In state enterprises the Party committee resumed control over personnel, especially over senior executives and directors. Many reform schemes were thus kept in limbo, such as the attempt at shareholding and price reform. This situation lasted until 1992, when Deng Xiaoping toured southern China and gave the reform a boost.[6]

That politics should stall the economic reform in 1989 was not surprising. In fact, the ideological debate on reform and socialism versus capitalism had continued for a decade after 1978. Although the reforms admitted the importance of the market as an economic coordinating mechanism, there was inadequate theory concerning enterprise management due to political taboos and rituals.[7] The market economy was still largely labelled as capitalism and the opposite of socialism. The central theme of decentralization during this period followed Mao's line of there being two main relationships: between the government and enterprises, and between an enterprise and its employees. The focus of the programme was aimed at motivating the state, enterprises and individual producers through a rational sharing of profits. Thus, enterprises enjoyed limited autonomy and the state remained in control.

The free market was limited to the less important products, most strategic materials and products were controlled by state planning quotas, and enterprises were subordinate to various government agencies.

Despite the progress of decentralization, the performance of state enterprises was not optimum.[8] Their share of total output value continued to decline, while, in contrast, non-state firms such as township, private and foreign-investment ventures had much higher growth rates. Table 2.2 compares the contribution of state enterprises with that of other ownership sectors. The proportion of total output value contributed by the state enterprises declined from 69 per cent in 1984, when the decentralization was introduced nationwide, to 54.6 per cent in 1990. In the same period non-state firms achieved steady growth, especially private and other ownership (such as foreign investment).

Up to 1989 there were four main areas of difficulty regarding decentralization. The first was that government – central and/or local – had administrative control over enterprises and much enterprise autonomy remained on paper. It was reported that enterprise autonomy was being hijacked by the relevant authorities in local government.[9] The second was the economic chaos caused by the change from a centrally planned economy to a mixed one with a market. There was a need to establish an appropriate market in which commodity transactions were not monopolized by the state and fair competition could be protected (*Economic Reference*, 17 November 1989; *Guangming Daily*, 11 February 1988). Reform of the pricing mechanism in particular was required, as the prices of strategic products were still under state control.[10]

The third difficulty was the relationship between the Party secretary and the director. In spite of the fact that the DRS was adopted in all state enterprises from 1988 onwards, there was no clear definition, in theory or policy, concerning the division between the Party secretary and the director. This was exacerbated by the different viewpoints presented in official ideology and management practice. In spite of the fact that Deng's ideology deviated from Mao's, he insisted that the 'Four Basic Principles' should persist. These were that China should adhere to (1) socialism, (2) the people's democratic dictatorship, (3) the leadership of the Communist Party and (4) Marxism–Leninism and Maoism. Therefore legislation that established the enterprise director as the decision-making authority would threaten the leadership role of the Party secretary representing the Party within an enterprise. It was noted that when the Enterprise Law was being drafted, a clear definition of the functions of the Party secretary and the director was deliberately avoided (Lian He, 1988). In practice it was largely dependent

Table 2.2 Contribution of different ownership sectors to total industrial output, 1985–90 (per cent)

Year	State owned	Collectively owned	Privately owned	Other*
1985	64.86	32.08	1.85	1.21
1986	62.27	33.51	2.76	1.46
1987	59.73	34.62	3.64	2.02
1988	56.80	36.15	4.34	2.72
1989	56.06	35.69	4.80	3.44
1990	54.60	35.62	5.39	4.38

* Refers to industrial enterprises with joint state and collective ownership, shareholding companies, foreign-owned industrial enterprises (that is, sole investment, joint equity ventures and cooperative ventures), and industrial enterprises invested in by overseas Chinese from Hong Kong, Macao, Taiwan and other places.

Source: *China Statistical Yearbook 1992*, p. 408.

upon the personal relations between the director and the party secretary, rather than formal regulations (Zhang Zhenhuan, 1987). Officially, the Party committee within an enterprise was seen as the leadership. At the same time it was stated that the director should play a 'central' role in decision-making, in an attempt to balance the relationship between business and politics.

The fourth difficulty concerned the poor qualifications of enterprise managers and the short-term orientation of state enterprises when pursuing profits (Li Lianzhong, 1987; Li Peng, 1988). The lack of qualified managers was regarded as one of the most serious problems. As Zhu Rongji[11] (1986, p. 55) notes: 'There is a gap in technology with the developed countries but the gap in management is even larger. So in some ways the training of managers is more important than acquiring technology from abroad'. In China's socialist centrally planned economy, management concepts carried a political stigma (Battat, 1986),[12] and there was a urgent need for management studies to educate professional managers (Warner, 1986, 1992).

Wu Jinglian and his colleagues (Wu Jinglian *et al.*, 1986) have made similar remarks, attributing the shortage of competent managers in China to problems common to centrally planned economies, where managerial decision-making followed the instruction and commands of the authorities. Others have noted that Chinese managers behaved more like administrative officials than business persons, pursuing bureaucratic procedures rather than economic interests (Yuan Baohua, 1989a).

The knowledge of management before the reforms did not include theories relating to market and finance and business strategies (Battat, 1986; Olve, 1986; People's University, 1980), and many managers had no conception of profits and the market (Liu Shibai, 1987; *People's Daily*, 20 June 1988).

2.2   INDUSTRIAL GOVERNANCE FROM 1984 TO 1988

State enterprises in China referred to those firms whose ownership in principle belonged to the people (*quanmin suoyou zhi*) and were administered by the state government. In reality a state enterprise rested in a complicated net of planning authorities, government agencies and the Party. Figure 2.1 depicts the hierarchy of industrial governance during the reform period.

As stated in Chapter 1, at the top of the hierarchy were the central government agencies. Of these the SPC was the most important with regard to economic administration. Below the SPC were two central government ministerial categories: industrial – those involved in production or services relating to a specific industrial sector; and functional – those involved in supervising and legislating economic practices. The local governance structure was similar to the central. The economic institutions in Beijing consisted of the Municipal Planning Commission (MPC), the Municipal Economic Commission (MEC) and industrial and regulatory bureaux.

A unique feature of this economic institutional setting in China was its matrix relations with enterprises, which formed a multilevel tier of supervision (Granick, 1990). Each of the local economic agencies had two higher authorities. The first was the local government, which had direct administrative authority over local commissions and bureaux in aspects of task assignment and personnel appointment. The other was an agency within the central government with the same function. The local agencies had a reporting line to the central ones. For example the MPC had a direct connection with the SPC and received instructions and technical advice. The Municipal Machine Building Bureau was directly accountable to the Ministry of Machine Building. The bureau received regulations/policies from the ministry, as well as technical assistance, with respect to the machine manufacturing industry. This relationship was called 'corresponding management' (*duikou guanli*).[13] The significance of this matrix relationship was to promote vertical communication between higher and lower levels. Local bureaux and

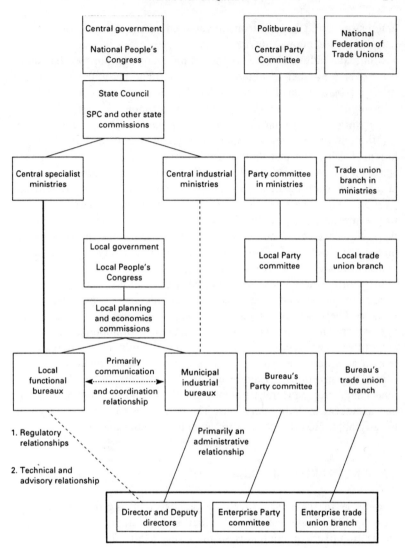

Sources: Adapted from Child and Lu (1990), interviews and documents held in the enterprises and municipal government, September–December 1988.

Figure 2.1 Industrial governance in the Chinese urban industrial sector

enterprises could benefit from understanding the central policies and decisions on economic development.

Municipal industrial bureaux, as administrative authorities, had authority over a number of enterprises. Their functions will be discussed in detail in Section 2.4. Functional bureaux, known colloquially as 'the mothers-in-law' (*popo*), could impinge upon enterprises on matters within their specialized regulatory purview. They specialized in taxation, auditing, industrial and commercial issues (such as the regulation of sales and distribution channels), pricing, investment finance (through the local banks), personnel matters (such as personnel regulations and keeping files on managers and party cadres) and hiring workers. While these bureaux were linked to central government functional ministries, such as the Ministry of Finance, their strongest links were with local government as a result of the decentralization of administrative power. Industrial and functional bureaux communicated and coordinated with each other.

In addition there coexisted political organizations, namely the Chinese Communist Party, the trade unions and the Communist Youth League. They had an independent system that paralleled the administrative hierarchy. These were, in descending order of importance, national committee, local regional committees, the committee in a bureau and that in an enterprise. These political organizations formed part of the formal organizational structure within state enterprises. Each had full-time staff, recruiting members among employees and supervising members and managers in daily operations. The enterprise's Party secretary was usually appointed directly by the bureau's committee.

2.3   ENTERPRISE REFORM IN BEIJING

Beijing, as the capital, enjoyed the prestige of being one of the three municipalities under the State Council's direct administration. Industrialization of the municipality began in the 1950s. By the end of 1988 Beijing was ranked as the largest producer of polyethylene, plastic and diesel engines, and the third largest of automobiles (Beijing MPC, 1991).

The reform in Beijing started in the late 1970s. In April 1979 the State Council selected three large firms in Beijing to test the decentralization programme,[14] together with another five enterprises in Tianjin and Shanghai. In 1979, 255 key enterprises in Beijing introduced the profit retention system (PRS), which had been extended to 342 enterprises by 1980.[15] The PRS was based on a complicated process involving the MEC and the relevant industrial/functional bureaux. The usual approach was for the industrial bureau to decide upon the proportion of profits to be retained by the enterprises. This would then be approved by the MEC and the Municipal Bureau of Finance. The retained profits were used for product innovation (40 per cent), welfare (20 per cent) and bonuses (20 per cent).[16]

In 1984 the municipal government selected nine enterprises to try out a measure based on the profit contract, which was the earliest form of the CRS in Beijing. This scheme underlined a clear division of responsibility and profit sharing between government and the enterprises. In addition to the CRS, the municipal government also tested a new taxation system in 10 enterprises. In early 1986 an unexpected decline in industrial performance forced the municipal government to seek a quick approach to motivating enterprises. The CRS appeared to be the easiest to implement[17] as the municipal government simply assigned a profit contract to each of its 14 industrial bureaux (*Beijing Daily*, 7 November 1988), and an industrial bureau in turn signed a contract with the firms under its authority. By the end of 1987 the CRS was being practised by all 425 firms under the municipal government's budget scheme, except for (The Capital Iron and Steel Corporation), which was contracted into the profit growth scheme. The CRS in Beijing was called the 'two guarantees, one link' (*liangbao yigua*). 'Two guarantees' meant that enterprises had to guarantee (1) a certain profit growth rate, usually 10 per cent a year, and (2) a certain increase in fixed assets through technological innovation. Enterprises were therefore obliged to carry out innovative projects assigned by their industrial bureau or the Municipal Science and Technology Commission. 'One Link' linked increases in employees' wages to profit growth. Enterprises' total expenditure on employee income, including wages/salaries, bonuses and other fringe benefits, was allowed to increase by 0.7 per cent whenever their profits rose by 1 per cent.[18] The implementation of the CRS was thus more complicated than the PRS and involved a number of bureaux.

First, an enterprise reported its average profitability over the past four years as a basis for the profit target calculation. Second, three bureaux, namely the relevant industrial bureau, the Municipal Bureau of Finance and the Municipal Labour Bureau, fixed the premium profit target as the contractual basis, then added the annual growth rate over the next three or four years, depending on the contractual term. The bureaux determined the budgets for wages and salaries and innovative projects. In most cases intensive bargaining took place between the enterprise director and bureau officials before the contract was finally signed. If any change was subsequently made to the contract, it needed the approval of all three bureaux. If an enterprise failed to complete its targets, it had to hand over its retained funds and halt pay rises. From 1984, parallel to the PRS and CRS, the municipal government selected 33 enterprises for the DRS. By the end of 1987 more than 90 per cent of enterprises had started to implement the DRS.[19] The political turmoil in 1989 interrupted the decentralization programme, but the effect was temporary. As most enterprises were under the CRS until 1991, it was difficult to insert political objectives into the contract. Giving greater autonomy to managers meant that the progress of the reforms was irreversible (for further details, see Chapter 8). Therefore the CRS and director dominance in decision-making continued after 1989. This will be discussed in more detail in Chapter 6.

2.4   THE SIX ENTERPRISES IN THE STUDY

This research aimed to study decision-making processes in state industrial enterprises. Six enterprises were selected as a sample for empirical study and data collection in 1985 and again in 1989. All were owned by the state at the start of the research. In May 1988 one of the firms, Automotive, became a joint venture with a Hong Kong company. This change in ownership influenced both the enterprise's organizational structure and its processes. It established a board of directors, and the industrial bureau was no longer the administrative authority. In areas of incentives and foreign trade, the enterprise gained more freedom than before. However the impact of the change on mainstream managerial activities was limited for two reasons. First, the Hong Kong company was actually a subsidiary of a Chinese investment corporation. Second, the Hong Kong partner only possessed a minority share in the joint venture and did not participate in management. For these reasons this enterprise was still viewed as a state enterprise.

Table 2.3 identifies, for 1985 and 1988, each enterprise's product category, total number of employees, financial profile, official size category and whether or not they produced primarily according to a planning quota or a profit target.

Three enterprises, Heavy Electrical, Audio and Electric Switchgear, were formed during the 1950s, when the 'socialist transformation' campaign was launched and the government took over the ownership

Table 2.3 Profile of the six enterprises

Product category	Date of foundation	Total employment		Sales turnover (Y million)		Net profit before tax (Y million)		Net profit after tax (Y million)		Official category	Size	Quota (Q) or profit (P) target	
		1985	1988	1984	1987	1984	1987	1984	1987	1985	1988	1985	1988
Automotive	1966	3883	5100	205	467	53.0	86.0	6.6	21.1	M	L	Q	Q
Audio-Visual	1973	2200	3000	183	418	13.0	13.0	3.1	4.1	M	L	Q	P
Heavy Electrical	1956	1869	1798	23	44	4.8	8.6	0.9	1.7	M	M	Q	P
Pharmaceutical	1973	957	912	27	43	4.0	8.6	0.8	3.0	S	M	P	P
Audio	1955	848	890	25	24	4.7	0.9	1.7	0.3	S	M	P	P
Electric Switchgear	1955	718	695	6	8	1.5	2.1	0.2	0.4	S	M	P	P

Notes:
* L = large, M = medium, S = small. Chinese state-owned enterprises are designated as large, medium or small depending on output, assets and number employed.

Sources: Data for 1984 and 1985: documents at the enterprises (September 1988), and Child (1987), Table 3.1. Data for 1987 and 1988, interviews and documents at the enterprises (September 1988).

of most industrial firms. Automotive was originally a plant for motor car maintenance and repairs. In 1966 the Ministry of Machine Building decided to establish an automotive production site around Beijing, and the enterprise was selected for this. Its production capability was expanded by taking over a small factory and by an investment grant from the ministry. Pharmaceutical used to be a subsidiary of a large firm. In 1973 the Municipal Pharmaceutical and Medical Products Bureau decided to separate it from its parent firm for the production of special health drinks. Only Audio-Visual was a newly established firm on a greenfield site, as in 1973 the Ministry of Machine Building and Electronics Industry planned a production site in Beijing to produce consumer electronic products, such as colour TVs.

Between 1984 and early 1989, the period covered by the two studies, the two largest enterprises, Audio-Visual and Automotive, expanded considerably in sales and employment and were officially 'promoted' from the medium-sized to the large category. Three other enterprises rose to medium-sized, making four altogether in this category. The large enterprises were more favoured by the planning system than the smaller ones. For example both Audio-Visual and Audio were under the supervision of the Municipal Electronics Industrial Office (as the bureau), but the former enjoyed a direct link to the ministry and the MPC, which gave it considerable support in the areas of investment, foreign trade, material allocation and technology. Medium-sized and small enterprises had to rely mostly on the bureaux to coordinate material supplies and give investment approval.

The six enterprises were under four municipal agencies, which were defined as industrial bureaux although they were called corporations or offices. During the interviews the enterprise managers still referred to these agencies as 'bureaux' (*ju*). Each enterprise was also linked to a ministry that issued central policies and plans, offered technological advice and approved strategic decisions on, for instance, investment. Table 2.4 indicates the enterprises' vertical relations with the bureaux and ministries.

The Municipal Electronics Industrial Office was established at the end of 1987, when the municipal government decided to develop the electronics industry in Beijing. The Municipal Automobile Industrial Corporation was established in 1982, based on the Municipal Automobile Bureau, following the State Council's decision to reform the China Automobile Industrial General Bureau into the China Automotive Industrial Corporation at the ministry level. The Municipal Machine Building Bureau was established in the 1950s. It was reconstituted

Table 2.4 The six enterprises, their industrial bureaux and respective ministries

Enterprise	Industrial bureau as the direct administrative authority	Respective industrial ministries of the central government 1985–88
Automotive	Municipal Automotive Industrial Corporation	National Automotive Industrial Corporation in the Ministry of Machine Building and Electronics Industry
Audio-Visual	Municipal Electronics Industrial Office	Ministry of Electronics Industry. After 1987, Ministry of Machine Building and Electronics Industry
Heavy Electrical	Municipal Machine Building Management Bureau	Ministry of Machine Building. After 1987, Ministry of Machine Building and Electronics Industry
Pharmaceutical	Municipal Health & Medicine Product Corporation	National General Health and Medicine Corporation
Audio	Municipal Electronics Industrial Office	Ministry of Electronics Industry. After 1987, Ministry of Machine Building and Electronics Industry
Electric Switchgear	Municipal Machine Building Management Bureau	Ministry of Machine Building. After 1987, Ministry of Machine Building and Electronics Industry

Note: In 1987 the two ministries of Machine Building and the Electronics Industry were merged to form the Ministry of Machine Building & Electronics Industry. Thus four enterprises – Audio-Visual, Heavy Electrical, Audio and Electric Switchgear – changed their ministries.

Sources: Interviews and documents, September–December 1988.

as the Machine Building Industrial Management Office in 1985, but took the bureau title again in 1987. The Municipal Pharmaceutical and Health Products Corporation, formerly the Municipal Pharmaceutical and Medical Products Bureau, was renamed in 1984.

It is evident from the study that the functions of industrial bureaux changed between 1985 and 1989. In the earlier years of the reform bureaux had administrative powers over enterprise management in the following areas:

- Assigning to enterprises state planning quotas on inputs and output, approving the enterprises' monthly and annual production plans and assessing the enterprises' performance against state plans.
- Allocating strategic resources, such as capital, to enterprises in accordance with state plans.
- Appointing all managers, including senior and middle managers, as well as the party committee secretary and party branch secretaries.
- Allocating and assigning workers and administrative clerks to each enterprise according to state plans, and approving personnel exchanges between enterprises.
- Designing or altering the organizational structure, and approving an enterprise's cooperation with other firms.
- Approving issues concerning operations (such as production plans and quality standards) and strategic areas such as investment.
- Assigning social and political obligations to enterprises, such as family planning, road-safety education, political training and community tasks.

The majority of these functions were removed with the implementation of the decentralization programme after 1985. In 1988 the administrative powers of the industrial bureaux were concentrated in the following areas:

- Applying local industrial development plans and specific policies concerning industrial sector management. Industrial bureaux were also responsible for drawing up one-year operational plans, including industrial outputs, financial budgets, technological innovation, human resource management and foreign trade.
- Administering enterprises, including appointing enterprise directors and the party secretary; supervising enterprise operation and performance; allocating resources; promoting research and technology within enterprises; implementing state plans; and assigning political tasks and other social obligations.

- Coordinating with other bureaucratic agencies. For example an industrial bureau had to communicate with the labour bureau regarding human resource management. Moreover some decisions, such as investment in a new factory, required the approval of the industrial bureaux and regulatory bureaux.
- Establishing a communication channel between enterprises and state government. A bureau was the channel for reporting enterprise performance to the government and transmitting government policies and documents to enterprises.

In political matters the bureaux Party committees directly supervised the activities of the party organizations in enterprises and reported to the MPC. The bureaux also had trade unions and Youth League committees (under the leadership of the municipal trade unions and the municipal Youth League committee), which managed the trade union branches and Youth League committees in enterprises. They also carried out social activities such as family planning, social security, pension schemes, education and training tasks. These interwoven relationships formed complicated societal networks. As an official in the Municipal Electronics Industrial Office said during an interview:

Although everyone wants to dismiss the industrial bureau, it is very difficult to do so. Without approval first being given by the industrial bureau, none of the other [regulatory] bureaux, such as pricing, labour and personnel, would be willing to deal directly with an issue raised by an enterprise. A bureau only talks to another bureau of the same level. On the other hand, an industrial bureau is very important for transmitting and transferring information and policies from government to enterprises and reporting enterprise statistics to the government. It [the bureau] is an important link to connect the government and enterprises.

As well as the industrial bureaux, enterprises had two other important contact networks, similar to the phenomenon of 'corresponding management' described previously. One was a direct link to the ministry that commanded new product development and controlled the technological standards of products. Both Heavy Electrical and Electric Switchgear, for instance, had to follow their ministry's blueprints for product design. The relevant ministries also allocated strategic resources, including raw materials, information, investment budgets and foreign trading opportunities, all of which were beyond the bureaux' scope.

Table 2.5 Functions and responsibilities of the regulatory bureaux

Name of bureau	Functions and responsibilities during 1985 and 1988
Municipal Labour Bureau	Local labour policy making, approval of workers moving into or out of the municipality, allocation of labour quotas and assignment of the total number of employees in each state enterprise, certification of technical grading to workers and control over the local wage budget
Municipal Personnel Bureau	Management of clerical and administrative staff, including managers and technicians within state enterprises, allocation of university graduates and assignment of technical human resources to enterprises, certification of administrative grading and control over the local salary budget
Municipal Pricing Bureau	Local price policy making, approval of price increase applications when the product was subject to state plans, monitoring and supervising prices within local markets
Municipal Bureau of Finance	Making local financial policy and budgets, collecting local revenue, approving special expenses concerning local development products and monitoring enterprises' financial performance
Municipal Audit Bureau	Auditing economic units and monitoring expenses occurring within enterprises
Municipal Industry and Commerce Bureau	Making local policies on business development, approving business licenses, supervising enterprise operations and monitoring enterprise performance
Municipal Construction Planning Bureau	Making local city construction and development plans, approving construction projects

Source: Interviews at the enterprises, October 1988.

Thus an enterprise with strong links to a ministry enjoyed supplies provided by the ministry, and thus gained access to the national market across municipal boundaries.

The other contact was the supervisory relationship with regulatory bureaux that acted as functional authorities with regard to public interest and societal obligations. Regulatory bureaux had no enterprises or production units, but instead had regional and district branches. The most important regulatory bureaux regarding economic administration are listed in Table 2.5.

Enterprise managers in functional areas such as finance reported performance data to their respective bureaux and received instructions. A regulatory bureau had the right to intervene in an enterprise's operation. For instance the appointment or dismissal of a functional manager within an enterprise required the consent of the relevant regulatory bureau.

2.5 MANAGEMENT SYSTEMS WITHIN THE SIX ENTERPRISES

Internal management of the enterprises studied had three strands, namely the director's administration, the Party organization and the Workers' Congress. The directors of the six enterprises were appointed between 1982 and 1986, and all had a university education and experience in industry. Their backgrounds are presented in Table 2.6.

The directors of Automotive and Pharmaceutical had been brought in from outside. The other four had been promoted from the Party secretary, or deputy positions in production or technology. Except for the director of Electric Switchgear, all were Party members and par-

Table 2.6 Personnel background of the enterprise directors, 1984–88

Enterprise	Date of appointment	Previous position	Education	Political background
Automotive	1984	Head of personnel department in the bureau	University degree	Deputy secretary of the Party committee
Audio-Visual	1986	Party secretary	University degree	Secretary of the Party committee
Heavy Electrical	1984	Deputy director of production	University degree	Deputy secretary of the Party committee
Pharmaceutical	1982	Deputy director of technology in another pharmaceutical factory	University degree	Deputy secretary of the Party committee
Audio	1983	Deputy director of production	University degree	Member of the Party committee
Electric Switchgear	1983	Deputy director of technology	University degree	Non-Party member

Source: Interviews held in the enterprises, October 1988.

ticipated in the Party committee. In 1986 the six enterprises adopted the DRS – prior to this the directors had been under the leadership of the Party committees. Through the DRS the directors were granted the following responsibilities, according to municipal government policy:

- Drawing up operational plans, including production, purchasing, sales, human resources, technological innovation and business development.
- Appointing and promoting/demoting middle and senior managers.[20]
- Recruiting workers and staff, however the dismissal of workers had to be approved by the labour bureau.
- Allocating rewards and bonuses.
- Designing and/or changing the organizational structure and establishing the required departments.
- Policy making in the areas of purchases, sales and prices, and selecting suppliers and customers.
- Using retained profits and other internal funds for production development and welfare.
- Disposing of redundant assets.
- Forming groups or affiliations with other enterprises.

Each director had four or five deputy directors with a division of responsibility for production, administration, personnel and labour management, technology and finance. Organizational structure will be discussed further in Chapter 6.

In 1986 and 1987 the six enterprises adopted the CRS and their directors signed a profit contract with the relevant bureaux. But Automotive later became a joint venture and the CRS was abandoned. The content and duration of contracts in the remaining enterprises are presented in Table 2.7.

Apart from Pharmaceutical's contract, which was for a three-year term, the others lasted four years. The enterprise directors were responsible for profitability, whilst the bureaux had no right in theory to intervene in enterprise management. In most cases the annual profit was required to have a growth rate, but in the case of Electric Switchgear it was different. The municipal government decided to take over a piece of land from the firm, and agreed to reduce its profit target as compensation. For this reason the enterprise achieved a smaller profit target in 1990 than in previous years.

As well as the directors' administrative system, there were two very important political organizations: the Party and the Workers' Congress. The relationship between the directors and the party secretaries will

Table 2.7 Content of the CRS in five enterprises

Enterprise	Date of contract signing	Contract term (years)	Profit target in the contract (Y million)			
			First year	Second year	Third year	Fourth year
Audio-Visual	1987	4	33.0	37.0	41.0	46.0
Heavy Electrical	1986	4	4.30	4.50	4.70	4.70
Pharmaceutical	1987	3	2.50	2.70	3.00	–
Audio Electric	1987	4	0.60	0.60	0.60	0.60
Switchgear	1987	4	0.87	0.92	0.98	0.94

Note: Automotive became a joint venture in 1988 and was not under the CRS.

Sources: Interviews and documents held in the enterprises, March 1989.

be discussed in Chapter 6. The Workers' Congress, according to the Enterprise Law, was the highest constitutional coalition to decide important and strategic issues concerning enterprise management. In reality it was a conference-like body that held annual mass assemblies or biannual meetings, in which the directors reported on the performance of the previous year and proposed targets for the following year. Its daily operations were performed by the trade union branches, which also assisted the party. The relationship between the directors, Party, Workers' Congress and trade unions is depicted in Figure 2.2 overleaf.

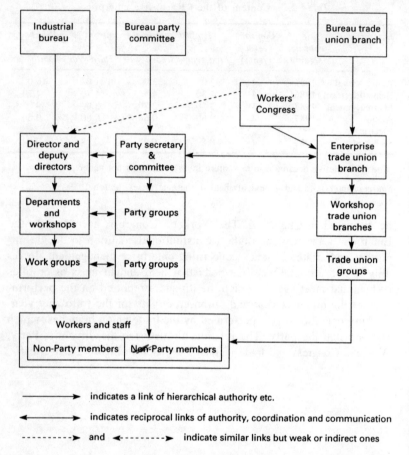

Sources: Interviews and documents at the enterprises, September–December 1988.

Figure 2.2   Internal management systems: director, Party, trade unions and Workers' Congress

3 Purchase Decision-Making: Raw Materials

3.1 ECONOMIC CONTEXT OF THE PURCHASE OF RAW MATERIALS

In the classical model of a centrally planned economy enterprises acted according to commands, usually referred to as 'plan quotas', issued by a planning authority, which in China could be the SPC, a ministry or an industrial bureau. Enterprises received supplies from an authority, arranged production and then delivered their output directly to the authority. Therefore an exchange relationship was organized vertically along the planning hierarchy, and there was no need for transactions at the horizontal level between enterprises and their suppliers and customers, as every aspect of input and output was coordinated and controlled by the planning authority.

Based on this model, in China raw materials and products, generally defined as 'goods' (*wuzi*), were categorized into two main groups, plan goods (*jihua nei fenpei wuzi*) and non-plan goods (*fei jihua fenpei wuzi*). The plan goods consisted of three categories. Category I comprised 'uniform goods' (*tongpei wuzi*), which were administered by the SPC and allocated by the state plan through the State Bureau for the Supply of Raw Materials. Category II comprised 'ministry goods' (*buguan wuzi*), under a central industrial ministry that organized supply, production and distribution. Category III comprised 'local goods' (*difang fenpei wuzi*) (cf. People's University 1980, Chapter 15), which were managed by local governments and ordered by the local planning commission and industrial bureaux. Non-plan goods were daily commodity products and unimportant materials, which were produced and distributed by the enterprises.

The government controlled plan goods in two ways. First, an annual production plan within an enterprise was limited to a ministry or bureau plan that was part of the state plan coordinated by the SPC. Second, the price of and distribution channels for the plan goods were also set by the planning authorities.[1] Thus an enterprise arranged its production plan according to plan quotas assigned by a ministry or bureau, received supplies from the relevant authorities and handed over all its products to the authority. The authority then allocated these products to other enterprises as customers.

This highly hierarchically coordinated production model was gradually dismantled during the reform. During the early 1980s the SPC began to relax its intervention in enterprise production by decreasing the number of products under state plan and concentrating its control on a few strategic products. From 1980 to 1985 the number of product categories subject to the SPC's plan decreased from 120 to 60 (Department of Institutional and Legal Reform of the SPC, 1988). In 1988 state control was reduced to 29 strategic materials, including cement, steel, petroleum and key chemicals (Wu Zhenkun and Chen Wentong, 1993). The majority of enterprises, therefore, were no longer subject to plan quotas for their production tasks. Yet their supplies were no longer ensured by planned quotas of inputs, and the exchange relationship was transferred from direct coordination with the planning authority to selected suppliers and customers in the market. According to a survey of 429 industrial enterprises, conducted by the China Economic System Reform Research Institute, the average share of market-purchased strategic materials increased from 16.4 per cent in 1984 to 43.8 per cent between January and June 1985 (Fan Qimiao, 1989, p. 16).

Since planning authorities such as ministries and bureaux no longer received or delivered goods and products, invoices were issued as plan quotas to specific enterprises. Enterprises were allowed to participate in an annual trade fair organized by the relevant ministry or bureau, through which they ordered supplies according to invoices. This system gave the enterprises a degree of freedom to select their own suppliers, according to the quality and delivery requirement. There was still no choice between prices because all prices were fixed by the state.

In principle the system would have worked if the suppliers had accepted the invoices as commands of the state plan. In reality it was more complicated because of a mix of state plans and imperfect markets. From 1985 the majority of products, especially those made of primary materials, had a dual price, which will be discussed in detail in the next chapter. If a producer fulfilled the state target it was allowed to sell all goods – raw materials or products – that exceeded the state quotas – the 'above-quota products'. A state regulation decreed that above-quota products could be sold either at state trade fairs or to approved production material exchange centres, subject to floating prices. In order to encourage production, floating prices were higher

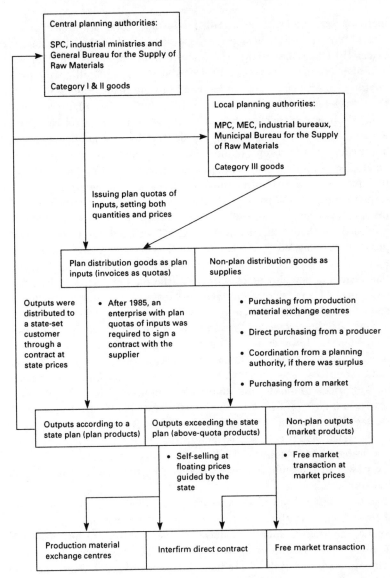

Source: Interviews held in the enterprises, September–December 1988.

Figure 3.1 Transaction relationships between plan and outside plan inputs/outputs

than state-set prices. A steel mill, for instance, was allowed to sell its above-quota products at a price 2 per cent higher than the state-set prices (Li Guang-an, 1988). These above-quota products, together with non-plan products, were usually referred to as 'self-selling products' (*zixiao chanpin*) and were not included in state plans. Figure 3.1 shows the transaction relationship between plan and outside-plan products.

This complex relationship between state, markets and enterprises caused uncertainty in purchasing. During the decentralization programme, when a ministry or bureau representing the state issued a plan instructing an enterprise to produce a specific product, it also had to issue an invoice of inputs to secure supplies for the enterprise. The enterprise had the right to refuse a ministry's or bureau's plan and sell its products on the market rather than to state-set customers if these invoices were not provided. In theory the invoices should have been equivalent to state production plans, so that every producer with state plans should have received its supplies from the state distribution network. But in reality the system broke down, resulting in friction between suppliers and customers. There was a shortage of most of the strategic materials subject to plan quotas, such as steel and non-ferrous metal products.

Since demand exceeded the plan quotas, suppliers had greater power than buyers. However if a supplier followed a state plan to sell its products to a state-set customer, the transaction was carried out under state-set prices, and these were much lower than both floating and market prices. Naturally the supplier was motivated to sell in the market for a higher profit margin, unless the state could effectively penalize the enterprise for ignoring the state plan. But this rarely happened as the relationship between an enterprise and its authority was negotiation-based (cf. Montias, 1988), and as decentralization progressed the power of the authority was weakened particularly if it was a central ministry.

Because after 1985 most enterprises had few or no plan quotas for their supplies, supplies could not be secured by plan invoices. Forced to seek alternative sources, enterprises were willing to buy materials at higher prices, competing with the state-set customers. A supplier with strategic materials or products was more likely to reject the state plan and sell its goods according to market prices and/or shift its production to products of high profitability. As Zhang Pan and Zhang Wenzhong (1989, p. 11) noted:

In times of high inflation, state plans were considerably weakened. Because plan supplies could not be secured or delivered in time or in the right quantities, enterprises found it difficult to complete their mandatory outputs in accordance with state plans. In such a situation, even those enterprises that usually carried out state plans honestly and loyally were forced to transfer their mandatory plan to the market, or raise the prices of these outputs through 'agreements' with buyers in order to compensate for losses incurred by increased costs of materials.

Firms with plan invoices for supplies faced problems because no supplier was prepared to follow the state plan. Rather the suppliers ignored state-set prices and quoted market prices. In effect this state plan–market mix resulted in increased supply prices. In the first half of 1988 the price index of production materials rose by 2 per cent per month (Wang Dayong, 1989). In 1986 the market price of steel products ranged between 50 and 280 per cent above the plan prices. From 1979 to 1986 the accumulated marginal revenue from price increases for about 200 strategic materials was as high as 24 billion yuan (Wen Guifang, 1989). In a survey conducted by the Bank of China in the first quarter of 1988, 89 per cent of directors of important large enterprises believed that the price of raw materials would keep rising, and 95 per cent feared a shortage of working capital in the future (Wang Dayong, 1989).

When the price of raw materials shot up, enterprises attempted to protect their profitability in two ways. The first was to increase their stock of materials in order to secure production. This in turn led to a further shortage of strategic materials in the market, and also caused a shortage of working capital, forcing banks to tighten credit to firms. The second was to increase their product prices, which triggered further inflation in commodity markets. However the purchase of supplies was regarded as a critical issue by directors.[2]

In a survey in Liaoning province, 89 per cent of enterprise managers said that a shortage of capital, energy and raw materials was the most serious management problem. Of them, 40 per cent said that an increase in the price of materials was the most crucial uncertainty with which they were faced (Gao Xuechun *et al.*, 1989). In September 1989 at a conference in Beijing, representatives of 28 of the largest enterprises complained that a shortage of capital, strategic materials and energy was the most serious problem. Moreover they reported that their plan supplies were no longer guaranteed because the planning system securing their supplies had been partially jeopardised by suppliers' ignorance of the plan quotas. For example Luoyang No. 1 Tractor Factory only received 23 per cent of its plan quota of steel. Sichuan

No. 1 Textile Mill had received only half of its plan supplies to meet the quotas. To make up the shortages, the enterprise had to purchase the rest from the market, paying 75 per cent more than the plan prices (China Enterprise Management Association, 1989).

3.2   CHANGE OF PLAN QUOTAS IN THE SIX ENTERPRISES DURING 1985 AND 1988, AND PURCHASING DECISIONS

The MPC in Beijing reduced its planned items from 858 in 1979 to 137 in 1987, including 24 materials subject to the SPC's control. Likewise the Municipal Bureau of Raw Material Supply reduced its supplies from 256 items to 21. From 1984 onwards, nine production material exchange centres were established to exchange strategic metals, chemicals, timber, automobiles and machinery products (Ji Zongwen, 1988). This affected enterprises in various ways. Most medium-sized and small firms had no plan quotas at all, and their output was no longer subject to distribution by the state system. For these enterprises, whose supplies came from the market, an increase in raw material prices affected total production costs and caused a decline in overall economic efficiency. From 1985 to 1989 the total profitability of 14 municipal industrial bureaux declined from 2.67 billion yuan to 1.1 billion yuan, at an average rate of 9.7 per cent per year. This low efficiency was mostly attributed to the increased cost of materials and energy, which rose from 8.68 billion yuan in 1985 to 16.23 billion yuan in 1989.[3]

Of the six enterprises studied, plan quotas were still significant for two large firms, whose production was under ministry and bureau control. The other enterprises had started to rely on the market for their procurement and sales. Table 3.1 shows the proportion of plan quotas of inputs and output for the six enterprises in 1985 and 1988.

The degree of autonomy given to the enterprises in selecting suppliers and distributors varied. In 1988 a majority of Automotive's inputs and outputs were still under the National and Municipal Automotive Corporations. Audio-Visual, a key producer of TV sets, was subject to the Ministries of Electronics and Commerce and the MPC. The other four enterprises, all medium-sized, had no output quotas. As a result they had no plan quotas of supplies. An exception was Heavy Electrical, which obtained some supplies, such as silicon sheets, from the Ministry of Machine Building and Electronics.

For each of the six enterprises two purchasing decisions were investigated, the first in 1985 and the second in 1988–89. To ensure

Table 3.1 Plan quotas of inputs and products as a proportion of the total in the six enterprises, 1985 and 1988 (per cent)

	Supplies purchased from state plan quotas		Products manufactured for state plans	
Enterprise	1985	1988	1985	1988
Automotive	75	64	84	70
Audio-Visual	80	60	87	82
Heavy Electrical	40	40	20	–
Pharmaceutical	–	–	–	–
Audio	–	–	–	–
Electric Switchgear	–	–	20	–

Sources: Data for 1985: interviews held in the enterprises, September–December 1988. Data for 1988–89: interviews held in the enterprises, May–July 1989.

consistency of the data, these two purchasing decisions were selected for their similarity. For instance the type of input purchased was the same in the later decision as in the previous one (Table 3.2). Except for the two decisions at Pharmaceutical, whose supplies concerned farm products, the other decisions involved strategic materials such as plastics, steel and non-ferrous metal products. These materials were procured either directly from the plan quotas, as in the case of Automotive and Audio-Visual, or coordinated by an authority.

3.3 DECISION PROCESSES IN 1985

In 1985 enterprise decision-making on the purchase of materials had to be coordinated with the enterprise's annual plan, which was closely linked to the state plan set by the relevant bureau or ministry. As a consequence, purchasing decision-making was a routine procedure. At the time each enterprise reported its annual production plan to the bureau, complete with a detailed supply list. The bureau took responsibility for the procurement of most materials through its coordination with other planning authorities, including ministries, material supply bureaux and the MPC. In all six enterprises studied there was little interruption or delay. The standard procedure for approving an invoice took a week or two at the bureau level. The purchasing manager of Audio-Visual recounted the decision-making process as follows: 'Our purchasing [in 1985] followed the annual production plan approved by

Table 3.2 Purchasing decisions and their duration, 1985 and 1988–89

Enterprise	Purchasing decisions in 1985	Duration (weeks)	Purchasing decisions in 1988–89	Duration (weeks)
Automotive	Purchasing steel materials at the ministry's trade fair	1.5	Purchasing steel materials at the ministry's trade fair	2.0
Audio-Visual	Purchasing a package of components from the ministry's trade fair	1.0	Purchasing plastic components from a foreign trading company	6.0
Heavy Electrical	Purchasing copper materials from its bureau	2.0	Purchasing copper from a foreign trading company within the ministry	4.0
Pharmaceutical	Purchasing bee-farming materials from a trading company	1.0	Purchasing bee products from a distributor	1.0
Audio	Purchasing a quantity of steel rolling-tapes from its bureau	1.0	Purchasing steel rolling-tapes from its bureau	2.0
Electric Switchgear	Purchasing steel sheets from its bureau	2.0	Buying steel sheets from a supplier	6.0
Average duration		1.4		3.5

Sources: Data for 1985: interviews held in the enterprises, September–December 1988. Data for 1988–89: interviews held in the enterprises, May–July: 1989.

the bureau and ministry. Our task was to draw quarterly and monthly plans and report to the bureau, which transferred our requirements to other planning authorities. The MPC and Ministry would arrange supplies of inputs.'

In all six enterprises in 1985, the role of the planning authorities in purchasing decisions was vital. The ministry and/or bureau granted the supplies and then supervised the vendor–vendee relationship. Supplies were secured by plan quotas via invoices, and only a few suppliers refused to deliver the plan quotas. Because the bureau was concerned with the performance of its firms, it tended to balance supplies within its administration. Thus Heavy Electrical, Audio and Electrical Switchgear were able to obtain materials from the bureaux, in spite of the fact that they had no plan quotas of inputs. The deputy director of Electric Switchgear said:

> At that time [1985], we seldom contacted suppliers directly. Instead we drew up our purchasing plan, reported it to the bureau and then waited for the delivery. Only if our plan was not met by the bureau, would we start seeking supplies ourselves. . . . The market in 1985 was not so chaotic as in 1988. We could [in 1985] get some supplies from the ministries and bureaux. The suppliers and distributors were still bound by state regulations.

The stabilization of the external environment through the plan helped to simplify the internal processes of purchasing decisions. Operational plan making was delegated to a deputy director of production and purchasing, and generally directors were not involved, except for Pharmaceutical where the director assessed the quality of supplies and decided the input prices. Table 3. 3 outlines the involvement of the different actors and their functions.

Information on material supplies was strictly controlled by the planning authorities, possibly because of the imperfect market. Market information was less important to managers, since most transactions were conducted in the government-based system. It was evident that all the enterprises, except Pharmaceutical, sought information from their bureaux or ministries. It was imperative for managers to be in contact with the appropriate authorities in order to understand the progress of deliveries and prices.

Table 3.3 Involvement of actors and their functions in the six purchasing decisions in 1985

Actor	Number of decisions involved (N = 6)	Actor's functions in purchasing decision-making
External:		
Ministries	2	Granting invoice delivery of state-controlled materials, arranging delivery of supplies issued according to state plans; providing information
Industrial bureaux	3	Granting invoice of quotas, arranging delivery of supplies issued according to state plans, approving enterprise plans, coordinating with other authorities, selling supplies to enterprises and providing information
Internal:		
Director	1	Approving purchasing plans and deciding specific procurements
Deputy director	6	Assessing purchasing plans, participating in trade fairs, selecting suppliers, negotiating with suppliers and determining procurement
Purchasing departments	6	Drawing up purchasing plans, coordinating with the bureau, participating in negotiations with suppliers and selecting sources, determining procurement details under the plan

Source: Interviews held at the enterprises, September–December 1988.

3.4 PURCHASING DECISIONS IN 1988–89

Six purchasing decisions in 1988 and 1989 were studied in order to compare them with those in 1985. Although similar supplies were involved, it was noted that purchasing took longer. On average the time taken had increased from 1.4 weeks in 1985 to 3.5 weeks in 1988–89. The enterprises spent time seeking information or finding suppliers. For instance in 1988 Heavy Electrical spent three weeks gathering information to compare domestic prices with international market prices. Audio-Visual sent a team to the ministry for information, and it took almost five weeks for the managers to reach their decision as they had to analyse data on supply and prices. In contrast, in 1989 Pharmaceutical showed how quickly decisions could be taken. Its purchasing manager was forced to place an order within three days because its stock of supplies was running out.

Flexible Purchasing Plans versus Unstable Environments

The time taken to make decisions was closely related to the flexibility of each enterprise's purchasing plans and the instability of the environment, in which material supplies were scarce. As described in Section 3.1, as state control over material supplies and enterprise production were relaxed, and part of state supply was taken over by the market, enterprises became responsible for managing their own production and supplies. As a consequence they had a larger number of alternative sources of inputs. In 1988–89 there were five key sources of materials, as follows:

- Ministry trade fairs, via invoices.
- Local supply channels controlled by municipal government agencies such as bureaux and planning commissions.
- Long-term vendor–vendee relationships – for example a buyer could invest in a supply firm and acquire the right to first purchase, or could form an industrial consortium through which members enjoyed first-purchase rights.
- Imports from foreign trading companies that were subsidiaries of a ministry or bureau, on condition that the firm paid in foreign currency.
- Directly from the market, for example through production material exchange centres.

The degree of importance the enterprises attached to each source varied. Table 3.4 shows the results of a survey of the six enterprises in 1988. Two large firms still relied, directly or indirectly, on sources controlled by the planning authorities, but their situations differed. Automotive required a large quantity of steel products. Although the ministry issued plan invoices for the supply of these, at the trade fair the purchasing managers from Automotive found that most suppliers refused to accept their orders. One purchasing manager remarked:

Table 3.4 Importance of different categories of supply sources in the six enterprises, 1988–89.

Enterprise	(A)	Category of supply sources (B)	(C)	(D)	(E)
Automotive	5	4	4	1	1
Audio-Visual	5	4	3	2	1
Heavy Electrical	4	4	3	3	1
Pharmaceutical	1	2	3	2	5
Audio	1	4	4	2	2
Electric Switchgear	3	1	3	2	2

Notes: (A) supplies allocated by the planning quotas; (B) supplies from local planning systems, such as industrial bureaux; (C) special arrangements with suppliers in a long-term vendee relationship; (D) imported supplies through foreign trading channels; (E) transactions in the market. 1 = unimportant; 2 = quite important; 3 = important; 4 = very important; 5 = extremely important.

Source: Interviews held in the enterprises in May 1989.

I couldn't make a choice, even though prices were higher than state-set prices. This was because there were fewer suppliers at the trade fair. Some suppliers did not sell what I wanted. Therefore, as soon as I found a source of supply I had to buy. However there were some advantages in the trade fair, because I could conveniently meet some important suppliers at the trade fair. Otherwise, I would have had to travel across the country to chase up each of them personally.

The manager indicated that he was only able to obtain 40 per cent of his requirements at the trade fair. For the remaining 60 per cent he had to go to each important supplier whenever he needed materials. As a result the director of Automotive decided to buy shares in a steel mill so as to arrange special supplies.

Audio-Visual, due to the scarcity of colour TVs in the market, was the best organized of the six enterprises. The firm arranged a mutual exchange with its suppliers in order secure strategic inputs: it assigned some colour TV to its suppliers of TV tubes, who in return guaranteed supply. Moreover the enterprise had strong bargaining power with the ministries and the MPC regarding plan quotas of inputs, such as imports. This interfirm link as a guarantee of supply was also seen at Heavy Electrical. It maintained close links with the ministry and the bureau to obtain some strategic resources, but it also helped one of its silicon-steel-sheet suppliers to buy a property in Beijing, in return for a secure long-term supply.

Actor Involvement

The changes were also evident in the involvement of actors and their functions, as shown in Table 3.5. The involvement of the directors, except that of Automotive, in selecting and approving procurement had increased since 1985. Although in the case of Automotive the deputy director and purchasing managers attended the trade fair, they were in daily communication with the director to report details of the supplies and seek advice. In general, departments such as finance and production also participated in the decision-making process, thereby complicating the internal process. At Audio-Visual, for instance, as procurement was the responsibility of a foreign trading company the finance manager was involved in advising on foreign currency stocks. When the bank started to tighten control over credit, the directors were faced with a shortage of working capital. This, coupled with the increase in the price of materials, forced them to restrict spending on purchases.

One phenomenon was noted from a close examination of interfirm relations: external firms often provided information through networking. One purchasing decision at Heavy Electrical was triggered by a message from a factory manager, who advised the enterprise to buy some copper materials because he believed their price would increase. The purchasing manager then tried to obtain more information from the ministry. Another example is that of Pharmaceutical, whose purchasing manager said: 'The decision [to buy] was prompted by one of my friends in a company. He asked if I could buy some raw materials he had. He knew what I wanted. Although the price was high, I didn't have much choice, because we only had enough of the material for one week's production.'

Personal relations with suppliers were important: because strategic materials were in a seller's market, buyers had little power in selecting suppliers, and thus suppliers gave priority to those customers with whom they had a harmonious relationship. As the purchasing manager of Audio said: 'Steel tapes were often in short supply. There is no problem in finding buyers. So a supplier favours buyers according to his [personal] relations with them.'

Relationship with the Authorities

Perhaps the most dramatic change was seen in the relationship between the enterprises and their bureaux. Some ministries and bureaux had established their own trading companies, staffed by former officials.

Table 3.5 Involvement of actors and their functions in purchasing
decisions, 1988–89

Actor	Number of decisions involved (N = 6)	Actor's functions in purchasing decision-making
External:		
Ministries	3	In Automotive, Audio-Visual and Heavy Electrical, granting invoices for state-controlled supplies, approving enterprise objectives, coordinating with other authorities, selling supplies to enterprises and providing information
Industrial bureaux	1	Granting invoices for state-controlled materials, providing information
Other firms	2	In the cases of Heavy Electrical and Pharmaceutical, providing information
Internal:		
Director	5	Approving purchasing plans and deciding specific procurements
Deputy director	6	Assessing purchasing plans, participating in trade fairs, selecting suppliers and negotiating with suppliers, determining details of procurements
Finance department	6	Providing information of working capital and available financing resources
Production department	1	In Pharmaceutical, providing information on material stocks available for production
Purchasing department	6	Drawing up purchasing plans, coordinating with the bureau, participating in negotiations with suppliers, selecting sources and determining procurement details under the plan.

Source: Interviews held in the enterprises, May–July 1989.

The bureau of Audio-Visual and Audio had set up two business companies: the Municipal Electronics Material Supply Company and the Municipal Electronics Sales Company. Using their relationship with the bureau, the two companies were able to obtain strategic materials under state plans and sell them to subordinate firms at a profit. They were also able to use the bureau's status to order products from the firms at low prices and resell them in the market. These trading companies purchased 10 per cent of colour TVs from Audio-Visual through the bureau's quota at state-set prices and then distributed them at floating or market prices.

Other enterprises still relied, to some extent, on a ministry or bureau for coordination or information. Heavy Electrical's key materials were controlled by the state so the enterprise purchased them through the bureau, but unlike in 1985 the firm had to pay market prices or service fees. As the purchasing manager said: 'At that time [1985] we still relied on the bureau's protection. [In 1985] the bureau did not seek profits when it was dealing with subordinate factories. But now it has started charging us a 2–5 per cent service fee, and selling us materials at market prices'.

In all six enterprises a change in the role of the bureaux was noted. On the one hand the bureaux had started their own businesses, and on the other they maintained their authority over the enterprises. As a result, a close relationship with a bureau was vital if strategic materials were to be obtained. Electric Switchgear shared its office building with its bureau's trading company in order to exchange strategic materials. According to Audio's purchasing manager: 'Our relations with the bureau are very good, so they consider our needs when they get some plan supplies from the state'. Even Pharmaceutical, which purchased supplies from the market, maintained a good relationship with its bureau. As the purchasing manager said:

> The bureau understands more than we do. We only have contact with a small number of companies, factories and individual farms, but the bureau is different. It used to be a distributor before the reform, and collected orders from its subordinate enterprises. [Thus] it has details of enterprise inputs, such as the quantity and quality of each item. As it has contact with other bureaux and ministries, it knows what is happening in other places and nationally. Finally, it can anticipate what is going to become scarce, where controls will be relaxed and so forth.

The role of the planning authority as a source of information was particularly evident at Audio-Visual and Heavy Electrical. During the ministry's trade fair the managers of Audio-Visual received a message from the ministry staff indicating that the ministry was going to reduce its imports of a specific plastic material, which henceforth would be supplied by a domestic producer. The enterprise preferred the imported material because of its high quality. Audio-Visual's managers later visited the ministry to follow up this information with discussions, in addition to seeking information from the market. When the price started to increase the managers reported their findings to the director and recommended importing a large quantity of the plastic. The purchasing manager of Heavy Electrical also sent a team to collect information from the ministry, because the latter 'knew the international market'.

3.5 DISCUSSION AND SUMMARY

Purchasing is an important transaction and is closely tied to the economic context in which a firm operates. A comparison of the purchasing decision processes of the six enterprises in 1985 and 1988–89 illustrates that the partial market reform in China created a complex environment. While the enterprises in 1988–89 had more alternative sources of supply than in 1985, they faced the uncertainties of shortages and inflation. These changes gave rise to changes in decision-making processes in terms of time frameworks, the involvement of actors and their functions. Decision-making processes in 1988–89 had become more complicated, and purchasing took longer. Directors were more actively involved and had the power of final approval, whereas in 1985 most decisions had been taken by deputy directors. Also, more departments were participating in the process, providing information and advice.

However the key factor was the relationship between the enterprises and the planning authorities. The latter still played a dominant role in the allocation of resources, but in addition they too had started to trade. As a result the dependence of enterprises on the bureaux was important. Furthermore it was vital for the enterprises to be able to rely on information sources in the planning system, because market information was not so readily available. Therefore a mixed form of state planning and the market constrained not only material allocation, but also, and more importantly, it constrained the flow of information that was crucial to purchasing decision-making.

4 Price Decision-making: Economic Motives and Societal Constraints

4.1 PARTIAL MARKET REFORM AND A DUAL-PRICE SYSTEM

Before analysing price decision-making processes within enterprises, it is crucial to understand how the state exerted control over prices and what problems the reform programme encountered. Prior to 1978 the prices of most agricultural and industrial products were arbitrarily determined by the planning authorities. By 1978 more than 97 per cent of retail commodities and 100 per cent of industrial products had mandatory state-set prices (Zou Xiangqun, 1993). As Wu Jinglian (1992, pp. 206–7) notes:

> Under China's traditional socialist planned economic system, the mobilization of resources and allocation of materials were coordinated by administrative commands, which mostly applied physical amounts [such as tons as the performance measure]. [As a result], the price system was established, not according to the relationship between demand and supply, but dictated . . . by administrative commands. Prices of basic consumer commodities were determined for the purpose of securing basic living standards, and producers' prices were adjusted only to increase [state] revenue and/or decrease inflation.

One important reason for the mandatory state price stemmed from political and social considerations. The concept of price was seen as 'capitalist', and for a long time the majority of policy makers and many economists believed that a socialist economy was a product economy in which prices should be abolished.[1] With such a political ideology the leadership deliberately kept the price of agricultural products and consumer goods low in order to maintain satisfactory living standards (Tian Yuan and Qiao Gang, 1991; Wu Jinglian, 1992).

When the economic reform started in the late 1970s, price reform stood high on the policy agenda. In 1979 the State Council's Finance and Economic System Reform Office proposed a general programme of overall reform. In this proposal it was suggested that the state should alter its price controls. The task of the state would be to maintain its price controls over strategic materials, while most industrial products and consumer goods would be transacted in the market, where their prices would be determined by suppliers and buyers.[2] The aim was to seek a period of transition, in which the state could control the price of strategic products subject to state plans, and the market could play a limited role in determining the price of less important products. This compromise between state control and the market mechanism was accepted and developed as 'adjusting first, liberalizing later' (*xian tiao hou fang*) (Tian Yuan and Qiao Gang, 1991). From 1979 to 1984 the price reform started with prices being adjusted through the state relaxing its control over a handful agricultural products, consumer goods, transport freight and a small number of raw materials.

From 1984 the reform was accelerated with the adoption of the liberalization programme, which sought greater influence for the market. The dual price system (*jiage shuanggui zhi*)[3] distinguished three price sectors: (1) state-set prices (*guojia dingjiage*) for Category I and II products controlled by the SPC and industrial ministries (see Chapter 3.1); (2) state-guided prices (*guojia zhidao jiage*) or floating prices (*fudong jiage*) for 'above-quota products', that is, products exceeding plan quotas; and (3) market prices (*shichang jiage*), which applied to farm products and daily commodities.

The liberalization of prices was achieved through two approaches. The first was to reduce state control and to pass on price decision-making to enterprises as part of the decentralization programme. In May 1984 the State Council decided that enterprises could sell their above-quota steel, machinery and electrical products at floating prices 20 per cent higher than state-set prices. In January 1985 this 20 per cent limit was abolished, and the prices of raw materials and most industrial products were determined by the supplier and buyer. From 1986 the state further relaxed its control over the price of industrial consumer goods, such as textiles, bicycles, audio equipment, household appliances and black and white TVs. The proportion of state-set prices for consumer goods declined from almost 97 per cent in 1978 to 50 per cent in 1988. Over the same period, state-set prices for heavy industrial products were reduced from 100 per cent to 60 per cent (Wu Jinglian, 1992). Enterprise autonomy over price decision-making was influenced by the coexistence of both state and market prices, and the degree of autonomy was determined by the product category. If an enterprise's products were not subject to state control, it could decide prices. But this freedom was constrained if its products fell into state-control categories, or if they were allocated by the ministries. Thus price determination mechanisms were more complex than before.

The second approach was to give administrative power to local governments. By 1986 the central government had assigned 240 products (out of 998) to local authorities to administer (Wen Guifang, 1989). Local governments, on behalf of the state, were expected to guide the price of strategic products and supervise enterprise price decision-making, but this caused problems. Since regional economic development varied, the degree of local government clout also varied. In places where the market was more developed, local government intervention was far less. For instance in 1988 in Guangdong province, which established the earliest market economy, the local government controlled the price of less than 25 per cent of agricultural goods, 20 per cent of consumer goods and 30 per cent of industrial products (Zhang Zuoyuan, 1988). But in 1986 in Shandong province, where the economy was less developed, 38 per cent of all product prices remained under local government price control (Tian Yuan and Qiao Gang, 1991, p. 205). This uneven distribution meant that a product could have different prices in different regions.

From 1987 the radical programme advocating price liberalization was hindered by rapid inflation (Fan Qimiao, 1989). Because the prices of agricultural goods, raw materials, rail freight and postage were traditionally kept low by the state, as soon as state-set prices were relaxed, prices in these sectors increased quickly. By the end of 1986, 40 per cent of steel products had risen in price. From 1979 to 1986 on average steel prices increased by 7.5 per cent, equivalent to 2.25 billion yuan (Wen Guifang, 1989; Zhu Min, 1988). The price increases in raw materials and transport were then passed on as increases in production costs, triggering price increases and eventually inflation. In 1987 overall prices increased by 7.3 per cent. In 1988 the average retail price had increased by 18.5 per cent. Fear of inflation eventually led to panic buying in 1988.[4] This instability forced the leadership to abandon the liberalization programme and regain control over prices (Tian Yuan and Qiao Gang, 1991).[5] On 26 September 1988 the Third Plenary Session of the 13th Central Committee of the CCP announced it would 'remedy the economic situation' (Sun Jian, 1992), which signalled a return to state control in economic activities.

The main difficulty with China's price reform was the high degree of market imperfection and the intervention of state plans in price setting (c.f. Fan Qimiao, 1989). In 1988 the state was still relying upon two administrative systems to control prices. The first was the price regulatory authority. Heading this was the State Price Bureau under the State Council and the SPC. It made pricing policies and drew up regulations on price control. Local price bureaux were responsible to both the State Price Bureau and local government. Although a local price bureau had no administrative relationship with industrial enterprises, it had control over the price of all products. This enabled the price bureau to intervene in transaction processes and penalize those charging unlawful prices. In order to control prices, three formal procedures were established. First, any product price set by the state had to be approved by the authority concerned. Before 1985, approval was in most cases given by an industrial ministry or bureau, but later it was transferred to the price bureaux. Second, a floating price had to be registered at the price bureau. Third, market prices were required to be reported to the price bureau, which could examine or alter them if necessary. The price bureau's power is illustrated by the following example. In February 1989 the Beijing municipal government decided to recentralize price approvals and freeze any price increases.[6] As a result all price increases, including market prices, were supervised by the price bureau.

The second administrative system was through the industrial ministries and bureaux responsible for enterprise price formation.[7] Whenever an enterprise wanted to set or change a price, the ministry or bureau was obliged to audit the price proposal in order to judge whether it should be recommended to the price bureau.

Enterprise price decision-making, therefore, was part of a complicated network of regulatory and administrative authorities as well as the market mechanism.[8] An internal documentation process coordinated the activities of the authorities and the enterprises. Internal documents (*neibu wenjian*) were circulated to institutions and state organizations[9] through (1) vertical channels at different levels among planning hierarchies and (2) horizontal links with ministries and bureaux. These documents contained a wide range of subject matter, including state policies (*guojia zhengce*); regulations (*guizhang*) or administrative rules; commands/instructions (*zhiling/zhishi*) from higher authorities; specific decisions (*jueding*) taken by higher authorities on issues relating to lower-level operations; and circulars (*tongzhi*) or other contents for communication. An internal document could be issued by one authority or jointly by several. The documents were distributed to individuals, such as directors and/or Party secretaries, and organizations concerned with issues addressed in the documents.[10] In price decision-making, internal documents were particularly useful in circulating information on state policies, regulations and state-set prices. On 4 May 1985, for instance, the State Price Bureau (SPB) circulated an internal document on the control of colour TV prices. The next day the SPB and the Ministry of Electronics jointly distributed another document, curbing price increases for colour TVs. Both documents were distributed to local price bureaux, electronics industry bureaux, state distributors and colour TV enterprises.

In addition the state launched specific schemes to investigate illegal prices. In 1987 the State Council organized three schemes to examine prices nationally. These were (1) an audit scheme in April, when the Council sent teams to 16 large steel works to examine steel prices; (2) a mission on 20 May, when the Council assigned teams to 27 provinces and municipalities to examine the price of strategic materials; and (3) a national campaign in October to investigate finance, taxation and prices. The latter became an annual campaign and was an effective weapon in enforcing these issues. It was supported by a number of authorities, including the People's Superior Prosecutor and Court, the SEC and the State Bureau of Commerce and Industry. In 1987, 600 000 unlawful price cases resulted in penalties of more than 800 million yuan (Zhu Min, 1988).

Price reform during 1978–88 suggests that price determination was a balance between state control and market demands, and that state-set prices conflicted with market prices. As seen in Chapter 3, state price control was in most cases imposed on products that were strategic and/or scarce. In other words, state control applied to seller's markets where demand exceeded supply. In general prices in the seller's market were higher than state-set prices. Therefore, logically, enterprises chose the higher prices in order to maximize profitability. However the state, through administrative measures, could force enterprises to follow state policy. As a result, price decision-making could be limited by state intervention.

4.2   OVERVIEW OF PRICE DECISIONS IN THE SIX
ENTERPRISES IN 1985 AND 1988

Enterprise autonomy in price decision-making was dependent upon its product category, which in turn determined its price sector. With the

Table 4.1   Main product categories and their price sectors in the six
enterprises, 1985 and 1988

Enterprise	Main products	Product price sector 1985	1988
Automotive	Transport vehicles	State	State
Audio-Visual	Colour TVs	State	State
	B & W TVs*	State	Market
Heavy Electrical	Electrical equipment	State	Market
Pharmaceutical	Health products	Market	Market
Audio	Audio equipment	Floating	Market
Electric Switchgear	Switchgears	State	Floating

* Black and White TV sets were released in 1986 at floating prices, announced
by the State Price Bureau.

Sources: Data for 1985: documents and MBA project reports at CEMI in
1986 and 1987, interviews and documents held in the enterprises in October
1988. Data for 1988: interviews and documents held in the enterprises in
October 1988.

progress of price reform, more and more products were moved from
the state plan into the market. This happened in all six enterprises
studied, where the state relaxed its control over prices from 1985 to
1988. In 1985 all but Pharmaceutical had very limited price discre-
tion, as the majority of their products were set at state or floating
prices. Price liberalization, together with the decentralization programme,
brought greater autonomy in price determination. In 1988, except for
a transport vehicle produced by Automotive and the colour TV manu-
factured by Audio-Visual, all products made by the enterprises were
sold at market prices. Table 4.1 shows the price sector prevailing for
the main products of the six enterprises in 1985 and 1988.

In each of the six enterprises, changes in two price decisions for the
same products in 1985 and 1988 were selected for analysis. The results are shown in Table 4.2. These 12 decisions can be grouped into
three categories according to the rationale behind the price determination. The first was to set a price for a new product. In 1985 three
decisions (at Audio-Visual, Heavy Electrical and Audio) fell into this
group. In 1988 there was only one – at Audio-Visual, which had developed a new function for a current product and applied for a new
price to be set. The second was to alter an existing price according to
a cost–profit formula, the rationale being profit maximization. A total
of seven decisions fell into this category in 1985 and 1988 – three

Table 4.2 Price decisions in the six enterprises, 1985 and 1988

Enterprise	Price decisions in 1985	Price decisions in 1988
Automotive	An increase in steel products caused an increase in production costs. The enterprise then decided to raise its vehicle prices.	The planning department proposed increasing the product price, due to a cost increase in materials. The director asked for a new price to be worked out, and then submitted it to the bureaux for approval.
Audio-Visual	The enterprise developed a new colour TV. Before the model was put into production, a price was proposed based on the cost-price statement.	The enterprise developed a new function for the colour TV and then applied for a new price to the bureau and ministries.
Heavy Electrical	The enterprise followed the ministry's new product development plan and launched a new transformer. Then it fixed a price for the product according to the ministry's price formula.	An increase in the cost of materials caused an increase in production costs. The enterprise then adjusted its product prices.
Pharmaceutical	Managers decided to increase prices for greater profitability, as the sales of their health products were going up.	The finance department found that the price of packaging materials had increased. A new price was proposed and reported to the directors.
Audio	After launching a new model of audio equipment, the enterprise decided to set a price.	The enterprise was forced to reduce its price because of a price war in the market. The deputy director decided to sell the stockpile at a low price.
Electric Switchgear	A price increase for steel materials forced the enterprise to increase its price.	Salespersons reported the price increases of other producers. The enterprise decided to increase its price and seek permission from the price bureau.

Sources: Data for 1985: interviews and documents held in the enterprises, October 1988. Data for 1988: interviews and documents, October–December 1988, April 1989.

decisions each at Automotive, Pharmaceutical and Electric Switchgear, plus Heavy Electrical's price increase in 1988. These decisions were prompted by the increased cost of materials. The third was the necessity of surviving in a hostile and competitive market, that is, it was a response to market pressure. An example of this was Audio's decision in 1988 to reduce its prices in order to remain competitive.

These examples show that price decisions were taken for different reasons by specific actors with specific interests. But as their products were subject to both state control and the market, the role of the state must be considered. The involvement of the authorities in price decision-making provides an indication of state intervention. Table 4.3 lists decisions involving ministries and bureaux, and departments within the enterprises. Three trends can be identified. First, there was a reduction in authority involvement over time. In 1985 three decisions involved ministries and five involved bureaux, of which only Pharmaceutical was the exception. By 1988 this had reduced. Only one decision, that of Audio-Visual remained subject to approval from ministries, and decisions at Automotive and Electric Switchgear had been delegated to the bureau level. The three other decisions were taken by enterprise managers. The involvement of the authorities was directly related to product category. If the price of a product was state-set, approval from the state was needed for it to change.

The second trend was that the price bureau gained greater power over prices. As Table 4.3 indicates, the number of decisions involving the price bureau increased from one in 1985 to three in 1988. This suggests a shift of price control from the industrial authorities to the regulatory authorities.

The third trend was that both directors and deputy directors became more active. Compared with decisions in 1985, by 1988 deputy directors were more involved in price assessment and coordination with the relevant authorities. The finance departments played the most crucial role in all three categories of price decision by providing cost-price statements and assessing proposed prices. Sometimes other departments were involved. The technical department helped with decisions on new product prices, possibly because it reported costs incurred in new product development and was required to prepare cost statements at an early stage. Ironically, no sales managers were involved in price decisions in 1985, and only one at Electric Switchgear in 1988. This was partly because prices were seen as a financial issue rather than a marketing decision.

Table 4.3 Involvement of actors and their functions in price decisions, 1985 and 1988

Actor	Number of decisions involved		Actor's function in price decision making	Actor's relationship to three categories of price decisions
	1985 (N = 6)	1988 (N = 6)		
External:				
Ministries	3	1	Approval of new prices and price changes for state products	In all three, as soon as product under state-set prices
Industrial bureaux	5	3	First approval of product prices subject to state control	In all three types, as soon as the product was under state-set prices
Municipal price bureau	1	3	Final approval of products prices subject to local government control	Mostly concerning price increases of state-set prices
Internal:				
Director	6	5	Internal approval of state-controlled prices. Final approval of market prices	Price increase. But not in Audio's 1988 decision on price decrease
Deputy directors	6	6	Assessment of price proposals and discussion of the recommended prices with the director	Setting new prices, price increases and decreases

continued on page 66

Table 4.3 continued

Actor	Number of decisions involved		Actor's function in price decision making	Actor's relationship to three categories of price decisions
	1985 (N = 6)	1988 (N = 6)		
Finance department	6	6	Participating in price setting, mainly in price assessment and discussion with the directors	Any price decisions, including new prices, price increases and decreases
Technical department	3	1	Drafting price proposals in the cost statements of new products, and setting prices	Setting new prices
Planning department	–	1	Drafting price proposals	Price increase at Automotive
Purchasing department	–	1	Assessing prices according to material cost data	Price increases at Automotive
Production department	1	–	Drafting price proposals according to production costs	Setting a new price at Audio-Visual
Individual sales staff	–	1	Proposing new prices based on market surveys	Price increase at Electric Switchgear

Sources: Data for 1985: interviews and documents held in the enterprises, October 1988. Data for 1988: interviews and documents in October–December 1988, April 1989.

The change in state control affects the efficiency of price decision-making, as can be seen from a study of the time framework of the process. Table 4.4 compares the duration of the 12 decisions from the first formal proposals to final approval.

The average time taken for the decision-making process increased from 6.7 weeks in 1985 to 8.8 weeks in 1988. Two cases (Automotive and Audio-Visual) involved state approval and took longer. This is not surprising, as in 1988 the state tried to control inflation by freezing prices. But decisions taken within the enterprises also took longer, as in the cases of Heavy Electrical and Pharmaceutical. In these decisions the enterprises were also under pressure from the state. Two decisions in 1988 took less time. The one at Electric Switchgear was taken relatively quickly even though the price bureau was involved. The other at Audio took less time than before because the enterprise wanted to sell its inventory as quickly as possible.

The following detailed examination illustrates how state control and market demand affected price decision-making in three of the enterprises. The first was Audio-Visual, which had least autonomy in price determination as its prices were strictly controlled by the state. The second was Pharmaceutical, which was the first to open to the market, and its two decisions in 1985 and 1988 were determined by its market position. The third was Audio, whose first price decision was controlled by the bureaux, while the second resulted from market competition.

4.3 PRICES UNDER STATE CONTROL

Of the 12 decisions studied, the two at Audio-Visual took the longest and were the most complicated, involving a number of ministries and bureaux. This strict control stemmed from the state policy on colour TVs, which were in short supply. To avoid price increases, the state set both the production and the distribution price. In the case of Audio-Visual, 80 per cent of its output had been ordered by the Ministry of Commerce, which then distributed the TVs to its local wholesalers across the country. Another 15 per cent of the TVs were collected by the MPC and the industrial bureau. The remaining 5 per cent were sold by the enterprise as above-quota products. Both the state distribution and the enterprise sales were at prices set jointly by three central

Table 4.4 Length of time taken and decision activities in the 12 price decision processes in 1985 and 1988

Enterprise	Duration of 1985 decisions (weeks)	Brief description of activities	Duration of 1988 decisions (weeks)	Brief description of activities
Automotive	6	Four weeks for approval from the ministry, plus two weeks for registration with the price bureau	16	Three weeks for internal discussion and selection of different schemes, another four weeks for the approval of the industrial bureau, then nine weeks for the approval of the price bureau
Audio-Visual	12	Four weeks for the internal preparation of the price application, including the proposal design, and assessment, plus eight weeks for the approval of the bureaux and ministries	16	Four weeks for internal proposal, design and assessment, four weeks for the industrial bureau's approval, and eight weeks for the approval of the central ministries and the State Price Bureau
Heavy Electrical	8	One month for the approval of the ministry	6	About four weeks for internal discussions between directors and the finance manager, plus three weeks to ascertain the bureau's position on the matter

Pharmaceutical	2	Very quick approval – within two weeks of the finance manager's proposal	4	One week for the discussion between the finance manager and the deputy director, two weeks for other meetings with the director, and one week for the director's final approval
Audio	6	Two weeks for proposal and assessment, plus four weeks for the approval of the industrial bureau	3	The deputy director took three weeks from submission of the proposal to determine the price
Electric Switchgear	6	Two weeks for internal proposal, design and assessment, plus four weeks for the approval of the industrial bureau	8	Three weeks for the collection of customers' responses, three weeks to exchange opinions with the price bureau, and two weeks for the approval of the price bureau
Average	6.7		8.8	

Sources: Data for 1985: interviews and documents held in the enterprises, October 1988. Data for 1988: interviews and documents in October–December 1988, April 1989.

agencies: the Ministry of Electronics, the Ministry of Commerce and the State Price Bureau. This state control over prices continued from 1985 to 1988. Consequently the two price decisions at Audio-Visual had a similar approval procedure, as shown in Figure 4.1.

The activities relating to these price decisions can be grouped into four phases. First, the technical department drafted a proposal – a formal statement that addressed the rationale for setting the price. Second, in its proposal the department included a recommended price, based on a cost calculation. Third, the recommended price was submitted to the finance department for assessment, and both the finance manager and the deputy director examined cost details. Internal meetings were arranged and several discussions took place among department managers. Finally, the price statement was sent to the director for first approval, before being sent for final approval to a higher level.

What complicated this process was state control over prices. In the 1980s the huge demand for colour TVs resulted in an increase in the sales prices since supply was limited.[11] The state wanted to lower colour TV prices to a level the average family could afford. But this control had an unintended consequence: as demand was excessive, prices in the market rose much higher than the state-set ones. One of Audio-Visual's products, for instance, could be sold in the market 15–25 per cent above the state-set price.

Expansion of colour TV production was constrained by two factors. First, the state wished to avoid overinvestment in colour TV production sites. By the end of 1987 there were 57 major producers and more than 100 small factories. As none of them had reached a satisfactory economic scale, the state sought to improve the existing producers quality and productivity rather than open new factories. Second, colour TV components were imported, but the state was unwilling to spend its limited foreign currency reserves on consumer goods such as colour TVs. As a result the state attempted to intensify its control over both distribution and prices. This control became tighter in 1988 when the state tried to halt inflation. Since it viewed prices as the lever to maintain stability, the criteria for colour TV prices were based on political considerations. In the words of an official at the Municipal Electronics Industrial Office, the bureau in charge of Audio-Visual:

Regarding prices, we examine costs in detail and give our opinion. Yes, we understand that high inflation causes material costs to increase. Because profit contracts are signed between our bureau and

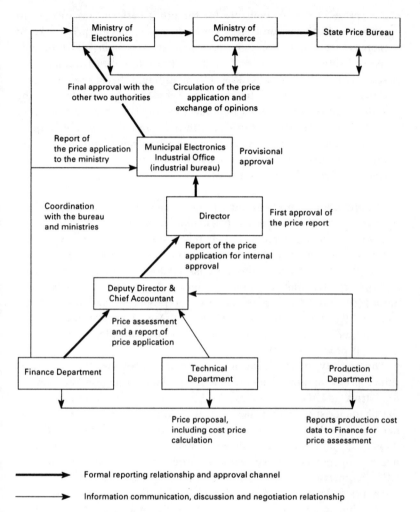

Formal reporting relationship and approval channel

Information communication, discussion and negotiation relationship

Sources: Interviews and documents held in Audio-Visual, December 1988, April 1989.

Figure 4.1 Decision-making process for Audio-Visual's new product price in 1985

enterprises, we're responsible for the profit performance of our enterprises. But, we can't say 'yes' whenever an enterprise asks to increase its prices. For some products, such as industrial products, the decision may be easier, because it has a less direct influence on society. But the case of colour TVs is different, because their prices remain sensitive to public opinion. People could complain to the state about the high price of colour TVs. In such cases, we are very careful. We compare our prices with those in cities outside Beijing. If our prices are higher than theirs, we will not permit a price increase. If ours are lower, we may forward a proposal to the ministries [applying for a new price].

This attitude of seeing a product price as an indicator of social stability rather than a sign of market demand was shared by the ministries. The finance manager recalled that the ministry staff were especially nervous when they heard the enterprise had applied for a higher price. From 1987 to 1988 the ministries issued four circulars emphasizing the control of colour TV prices. Internal documents were circulated among the ministries, bureaux, TV set producers and distributors, stressing the freezing of colour TV prices. Any change of price needed joint consent from the three agencies. These measures led to the lengthy approval process in 1988.

This rigidity of price control caused conflict, because the low prices ruined profit margins. This created a negotiating situation between the ministries and the enterprises. As Montias (1988) has noted, one of the characteristics within the vertical central planning system was its negotiating relationship, in which the enterprise could negotiate with its planner for task assignments and resource allocations. Audio-Visual's negotiating power was strengthened after the enterprise adopted the CRS, requiring the enterprise to sustain adequate profitability. In the 1988 price decision, managers argued with the ministries that their prices should guarantee an adequate profit, otherwise the enterprise would be unable to fulfil the profit contract. Many rounds of discussions were arranged for the purpose of examining cost details and comparing enterprise prices with those of other producers. In this complicated interaction with the ministries, 'keeping a good relationship with the bureau/ministry' was a popular practice and personal relations (*guanxi*), as an informal link, were widely used to accelerate the approval. Personal visits and phone calls were particularly useful in persuading ministerial staff to accept the enterprise's ideas.

Audio-Visual's decisions demonstrated how state policies directly impinged on enterprise management. It also suggested that the degree of state intervention could be increased in two circumstances: first, when a product was in a seller's market, where market prices were higher than those of the state; and second, when the economy became unstable and the state had to control the market. This was particularly true when the state attempted to reduce inflation by means of freezing prices. As a result it was expected that approval of price increases in 1988 would be more difficult than in 1985, even though approval was delegated to local government.

In the two decisions in 1988 at Automotive and Electric Switchgear, the power of price control was shifted from the industrial ministries to the bureaux. Automotive's prices in 1988 were administered by local bureaux, but this did not accelerate the procedure. As with Audio-Visual, approval took several weeks because, as a manager of Automotive recalled, 'In 1988 price increases were not liked [by the state].' This implied that the price increases in 1985 were more acceptable because of price liberalization.

The lengthy process in 1988 was also caused by the involvement of the price bureau, which added another element to state control. One manager put it as follows. In 1985 the enterprises only dealt with one 'god' – the industrial bureau. In 1988 they were faced with several 'gods', the industrial and regulatory bureaux. If any one of them had doubts about a price application, the enterprise had to start the whole procedure again with new cost statements. However a negotiating relationship was also evident. The public relations department in Automotive invited the price bureau staff to visit the production site, while senior managers also lobbied the MEC to coordinate with the bureau for approval.

The power of the regulatory authority could also extend to intervention in an individual price decision, even though the firm had no plan quota products, as seen in Electric Switchgear's 1988 decision. Its product used to be one of the ministry's products, but it was opened to the market after 1986. The managers thought the price no longer needed state approval, but the price bureau insisted on examining the case, asserting that approval was needed. Personal relations played a key role in speeding up the process. The deputy director was an old friend of a senior official at the price bureau. He used this relationship to ask his friend to 'supervise the case'. As a result it only took two weeks to obtain the bureau's permission.

4.4   OPERATING IN THE MARKET

It has been suggested that price decision-making in 1988 took longer, even in enterprises not under state-set price control (for example Pharmaceutical's products were open to the market and its prices were determined by demand and supply), so it is necessary to examine why this happened.

The strategic product at Pharmaceutical was a health drink. In theory the enterprise had the power to determine prices without interference from the planning authorities. During the 1980s Pharmaceutical was the market leader through improved product quality and a successful marketing strategy. Therefore its two decisions to raise prices were determined by its economic performance, and both were determined by the director without the involvement of the bureaux or ministries. These decision processes were not complicated in that only three actors were involved, namely the finance manager, the deputy directors and the director. Figure 4.2 portrays the price decision-making process in 1988.

The process was similar to the four phases identified for Audio-Visual. In the early stage the finance department drafted a proposal, then designed a price. This recommended price was later assessed by the deputy director, and finally approved by the director. There was no need for state approval. Consequently, after the director agreed to the new price it was circulated to the distributors. The difference between the process in 1985 and 1988 was the time it took: about three weeks in 1988 compared with two in 1985.

This extra time had two causes. The first was the enterprise's position in the market. In 1985, the enterprise enjoyed a market leader position, and the demand for its products exceeded supply. The enterprise decided to increase its price in the interest of greater profit. Therefore the process was rapid, as the finance manager later recalled, because the managers were eager to do it.

From 1986 its market leader position was challenged as the market was full of new entrants. The number of health drink factories had increased from about 150 in 1984 to more than 400 in 1988, and there were thousands of similar products in the shops. While producers wanted to lower prices to increase sales, an increase in the cost of raw materials in 1987–88 ruined profitability. The finance manager noted that the cost of packaging had risen by 24 per cent. He therefore proposed raising the price of the product to maintain profitability. But senior managers hesitated because it had become a buyer's market. Although the enterprise still provided the best-quality product,

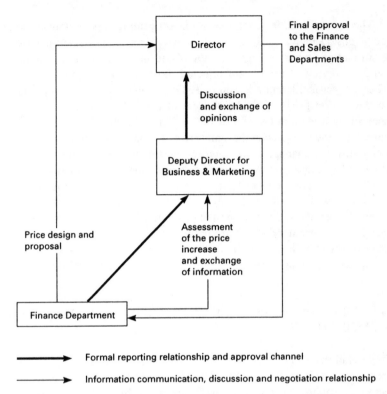

Formal reporting relationship and approval channel

Information communication, discussion and negotiation relationship

Sources: Interviews and documents held in Pharmaceutical, October 1988 and April 1989.

Figure 4.2   Decision-making process of the price increase in Pharmaceutical in 1988

its market share was gradually being taken over by other competitors. The directors were unsure whether the higher price would be accepted by consumers. Several rounds of discussions were arranged between the finance manager, the deputy director and the director in order to determine the market situation. As a result the price decision took longer.

The second factor was that the price freeze was tending to deter price increases and was making managers cautious. Although the product was at the market price, the managers wished to avoid being criticized by the media. As the deputy director of Pharmaceutical said, the managers were unsure what to do, as the state, especially the price bureau, could reject the new price if customers complained.

The fear of state intervention in market pricing was evident in other decisions. The authorities could interfere through the annual price examination, when a team of officials from the industrial and price bureaux reviewed prices and rejected those that were deemed illegal. Heavy Electrical learnt a lesson in 1987. The enterprise sold its products at the market prices with the consent of the industrial bureau, but the examination team at the end of the year insisted that the prices needed approval, thus requiring the enterprise to apply for permission. Consequently the managers were more careful in 1988. Before they decided to increase prices, a senior manager spent three weeks visiting each of the bureaux in order to ascertain the position of the state.

The above cases show that the enterprises were constrained by state control, even though they operated in the market. Although their prices needed no formal approval from the state, the state could force the enterprises to follow its policies through other measures, such as price examinations or an authority's rejection of individual prices.

4.5   PRICE DECREASE: THE ENTERPRISE'S RESPONSE TO A COMPETITIVE MARKET

The relationship between the state and enterprises in the buyer's market was noted by Byrd (1987, p. 254) as follows: 'Government responses to buyers' markets in China have been most striking in marketing. The government planning and distribution systems have essentially abdicated responsibility for procuring enterprise output, forcing producers to fend for themselves on the open market, with responsibility for sales of their own products (at least at the margin).'

As in the case of Pharmaceutical, where supply was excessive, competing firms could lower their prices to attract customers. In this context the state did not intervene. Of the 12 price decisions, only one was to reduce prices. This was the scenario for Audio's price decision in 1988.

The enterprise was under the bureau's control in 1985, when it decided to set a price for the stereo cassette recorder it produced under license from a Japanese company. In 1985 the product was sold at the floating price, and approval was given by the industrial bureau. The whole procedure took time, similar to other price decisions that involved the authorities. The product was in a good market during 1985 and 1986, but this changed rapidly after 1987 as the audio market became more unpredictable. Before 1984 the enterprise competed with just five other firms assigned by the ministry, but by 1988 there were more than 40 producers of similar products. If small factories are included, the total number of producers amounted to more than 300.

With so many producers, supply quickly exceeded demand and competition was vigorous. In October 1987 a number of audio manufacturers announced price reductions of 5–15 per cent. This started a price war. Audio found that its product was no longer so attractive, because for the same price consumers could buy more fashionable, updated equipment. In early 1988 distributors began to stop their orders. The enterprise's stock of finished goods increased rapidly, causing a shortage of working capital. Under such pressure the finance manager proposed disposing of the stockpile as soon as possible.

Coincidentally, panic buying raged across the country in the summer of 1988. Audio's managers saw this as an opportunity to get rid of their out-of-date products. It was in this context that the decision was made to reduce prices. The decision was made by the deputy director and the finance manager, although the formal procedure stipulated that price reductions needed the approval of the director. A few days earlier the executive committee had delegated power to make price decisions to the deputy director in order to deal with product sales. However the deputy director did not take immediate action, partly because a price reduction would also reduce profitability, and partly because he wanted to wait and see if the panic buying would promote sales. The decision therefore took almost three weeks.

There were also other considerations. The stockpile was finally sold to the enterprise's labour service company, a subsidiary employing the children of Audio's employees. The price was reduced to a very low level, which enabled the subsidiary to make a profit from the sales. As the deputy director said, the decision favoured those in the service company, who were 'our own people'.

In the buyer's market the enterprise became vulnerable when the economic environment was unstable. Unlike Audio-Visual, which delivered most of its products to the planning authorities, Audio had little help from the bureau. As one manager said, 'They [the bureau] did not care about the price decrease. Perhaps they thought it was good to reduce prices'. During 1987 and 1988 the industrial bureau tried to establish several industrial groups, affiliating subordinate factories. Through its administrative power the bureau ordered some leading firms to subcontract some business to those in a contestable market. This method was questionable. Audio joined one group, but each member still operated independently, gaining no benefit from the alliance. This kind of consortium aimed at internal protection was also found at Heavy Electrical, which became a member of a large industrial group based in northern China. Members decided to fix a price aimed at protecting their profit margins.[12]

4.6 DISCUSSION AND SUMMARY

A comparison of the 12 price decisions in 1985 and 1988 suggests that the decentralization programme increased enterprise autonomy with regard to price determination. This was possibly because of the relaxation of state control over prices, and the liberalization of the economy. This autonomy was, however, contingent on two related factors. The first was the price sector in which the enterprise product was located. The second was the demand and supply relationship in the market. Analysis of the 12 price decisions in 1985 and 1988 shows that the market mechanism became increasingly important in price determination, a conclusion consistent with Byrd's (1987) research. The expansion of the market changed the enterprises' position. From 1985 to 1988, firms such as Audio-Visual enjoyed a seller's market because of excess demand, but others, such as Audio, began to feel the pressure of vigorous competition. A price decision within an enterprise was therefore connected to its market situation.

The case studies also showed that the state was still able to limit enterprise autonomy. This intervention was largely seen in the seller's market, where shortages pushed prices higher than state-set prices. State-set prices were dictated by command, based largely on social and political considerations. This intervention was exercised through the regulatory authorities' power to approve a price, and by the industrial authority responsible for product price formation. The enterprises limited by state control usually tried to increase their prices through negotiation and lobbying. Thus price decision-making became a complicated and lengthy process. The conflict between the state's social and political rationale and the enterprise's interests was the main problem in such decision-making.

At the other extreme, when supply was excessive the state left the enterprises to compete with each other. Byrd (ibid.) explains that this was possibly because the state wanted market forces to control production. Audio's case provides a contrast to Audio-Visual's. The latter had to negotiate to increase its prices, but the former was forced to reduce its prices and accept a loss. In enterprises such as Audio the role of the state was limited. Although Audio joined an industrial group its position remained vulnerable. Its price decision was made in order to survive in the face of strong competition.

Other enterprises used prices to protect their own profitability. Here state intervention was mixed with market forces. As Byrd observed, even in a seller's market where a Chinese firm had the freedom to set its prices, raising prices might not be acceptable if a firm wanted to maintain a long-term relationship with its customers or create a good image. This analysis was similar to that found in Pharmaceutical's case.

Analysis therefore suggests that price decision-making in China has not been a truly economic issue. Rather it has been a complex mix of social and political pressures, as well as a desire to maximize profits.

5 Recruitment Decisions

5.1 THE EMPLOYMENT SYSTEM IN STATE ENTERPRISES AND LABOUR REFORM FROM 1984

Economic analysis of recruitment in market economies assumes that a producer's decision to hire workers is for maximum profitability through the contribution made by labour (Reekie *et al.*, 1991), and the main mechanism for meeting a producer's demand for labour is coordination of the labour market (Torrington and Hall, 1987). Recruitment starts with a need for manpower as a result of expansion or job vacancies. In reality, as personnel management theory has noted, recruitment decision-making can be complicated because social, political and geographical factors, as well as economics, influence the process.

The idea that recruitment is a result of market coordination between the demand for and supply of labour may not be applicable in a socialist command economy. A handful of empirical studies and data from countries in Eastern Europe and China suggest that employment systems in command economies differ significantly from the demand–supply relationship in the market. Rather, recruitment decision processes result from state planning (Smith and Thompson, 1992). Recruitment is regarded as a political process that relies upon the state and the Party apparatus. Contrary to the market, where both employer and employee have some degree of autonomy in job selection, in a socialist economy an enterprise's demand for labour is constrained by the plan quota allocation. As manpower needs may not be met by the quota, managers are motivated to overstate their requirement for workers in order to deal with the potential uncertainties of labour shortages. This gives rise, as Thompson and Smith (1992) note, to a waste of human and technical resources.

The unique characteristic of socialist labour management draws attention to the link between recruitment and the state in China. As China has the largest population in the world, for a long time the government adhered to a strategy of 'high employment, low salary' (*gaojiuye, digongzi*),[1] for the purpose of maintaining stability and providing acceptable living standards. Chinese labour institutions consisted of three systems (Dang Xiaojie *et al.*, 1991). The first was *labour planning*. The state planning authorities assigned a plan quota to each state enterprise regarding (1) the number of employees, and (2) the total wage/salary budget (Wang Aiwen, 1991). The second was the *employment system*. Before 1987 this system guaranteed most workers in state enterprises permanent employment and life-long security. The third system was the *employee management system*, which had two subsystems. Manual workers were administered by labour authorities, whilst managers, technicians and office staff were registered at a personnel bureau. An employee's appointment, wage/salary, rewards, welfare, medical care and retirement were all regulated by the state.

These three systems were closely linked to central planning. Heading the institutional structure was the Ministry of Labour and Personnel as the central authority in labour administration, reporting to the State Council and the SPC. Below this were local labour and personnel bureaux, which were responsible to both the central ministries and local government. Following the state policy of high employment, these labour/personnel authorities centralized all employment decision-making. Recruitment was conducted according to the state employment plan that assigned employees to enterprises. Thus the state, rather than the enterprise manager, controlled recruitment. This procedure, coordinated by the bureaux, became extremely rigid. Any change in an employee's position within the enterprise or his or her leaving the work unit needed the bureau's approval.

The high employment policy and the rigidity of the bureaucratic procedure caused problems, in particular a waste of human resources and low productivity. Two main drawbacks were recognized, namely the iron rice bowl (*tie fanwan*), where guaranteed life-long employment failed to motivate workers to improve their performance, and 'eating from one big pot' (*daguo fan*), referring to equal wages and bonus allocation, which likewise discouraged productivity. From the 1950s several attempts were made to reform the employment system. In 1956 a proposal called for the adoption of a contract labour system.[2] In the early 1960s, Liu Shaoqi's 'Two Labour Systems' (*liangzhong yonggong zhidu*) was published. However neither of these proposals was put into practice, due to political events such as the Great Leap Forward and the Cultural Revolution.[3] As a result, prior to the reform China's labour system was regarded as inflexible. As the World Bank (1985, p. 131) notes:

China's system of labour allocation allows individual employers and employees uniquely little freedom of choice – far less even than in the [former] Soviet Union and Eastern Europe. Until recently, all young people were administratively assigned to particular jobs – college graduates by the central government, secondary school graduates by local labour bureaux – with little attention to their preferences or the preferences of employers. The assignment was typically for life: with few exceptions (generally dictated from above rather than a result of individual or employer preferences). Workers could not move from one enterprise to another. Enterprises, moreover, were not permitted to discharge workers, even if they had more employees than they needed, and even if particular employees were habitually absent, lazy, or negligent.

When the economic reform started in the late 1970s it was proposed to delegate to enterprises the power to make decisions about employment. In 1979 the State Council published a number of policies on enterprises' right to decide recruitment and labour management issues, but this was stalled because of the government's fear of instability caused by unemployment. Compared with other reform programmes, labour reform was a relatively slow process. During the early 1980s labour reform remained on paper[4] because the state had to solve the unemployment problems of those who had been sent as youths to the countryside during the Cultural Revolution. The state then required enterprises to hire extra employees.[5] Progress in labour reform was halted until 1986, when the State Council published a set of four regulations:

1. Workers were to be recruited by the enterprises and the tradition of 'children succeeding to their parents' positions' (*zinu dingti*) was to be stopped.
2. The contract labour system (CLS) was to replace permanent employment. Both employees and employers were to sign a fixed-term labour contract. The labour authorities were no longer responsible for assigning workers and school graduates to enterprises, or for approving an employee's leaving and enterprise recruitment.
3. Enterprise directors were required to develop training programmes to improve workers' skills and qualifications.
4. Enterprise directors were to take responsibility for labour management, according to the enterprise's manpower needs, including both the recruitment of new workers and laying off employees.

These measures were critical in promoting enterprise autonomy in labour management. Managers began to enjoy much more authority than before. This autonomy was further advanced by the introduction of the CRS, and managers were now able to take recruitment decisions. In Beijing, for instance, after 1987 the personnel and labour bureaux no longer assigned plan quotas to control the number of employees in an enterprise, although they fixed its wage/salary budget. The expansion or reduction of workers, now delegated to managers, was called 'increasing workers without increasing wages (budget), decreasing workers without decreasing the wages' (*zengren buzeng gongzi, jianren bu jian gongzi*).

5.2 LABOUR MANAGEMENT IN THE SIX ENTERPRISES

In 1988 there were three employment systems in the six enterprises studied, namely permanent, contract and temporary. Permanent employment was divided into two subgroups: labour management in charge of manual workers, and personnel management for managers, Party cadres, technicians and office staff (Table 4.1). Although the CLS was introduced in October 1986, a large number of employees during 1987 and 1988 remained in permanent employment, whilst contract employment was limited to new workers recruited after January 1987.

When the labour reform started the enterprises had two main employment problems. The first was overmanning and a waste of human resources. When the CRS was introduced in 1987, managers wanted to reduce the number of employees by laying off those who were surplus to requirement (See Chapter 6 for further details). However, this was only part of the picture as there was a shortage of highly skilled workers. As a labour manager at Audio said:

> Senior workers have retired and young people are not good enough to master all the skills needed in die making or electrical engineering. This problem has existed for some years. Although the bureau asked enterprises to select surplus workers, they either lacked the skills we needed or were too old to be trained. Typically skilled and young workers were unwilling to work in state enterprises because of very low wages and poor welfare [provisions]. The only attraction was that we provided housing for workers.

Some enterprises, such as Automotive, felt that their technological innovation and product development was suffering from poor technicians. Therefore managers were under pressure to find highly skilled labour. To solve this problem the enterprise had two alternatives: recruit from external sources or develop existing employees' skills.

Table 5.1 Employment systems in the six enterprises, 1985 and 1988

Items of labour management	Permanent employees		Contract workers	Temporary workers
	Personnel (office staff, managers, and technicians)	Labour (workers)		
Employment term	Life-long	Life-long	Contract based	Contract based
Salaries and wages	Salaries set by the state, with 11 grades	Wages set by the state, with eight grades	Determined by negotiation between worker and enterprise	Determined by negotiation between worker and enterprise
Welfare and medicine	Covered by the state scheme	Covered by the state scheme	Covered by the enterprise	Covered by the enterprise
Pension scheme	Covered by the state scheme	Covered by the state scheme	Covered jointly by enterprise and employee	Covered jointly by enterprice and employee
Recruitment procedure	According to the state quota	According to the state quota	Determined by the enterprise	Determined by the enterprise, but had to be registered at the local labour bureau
Dismissal procedure	Required the labour bureau's approval	Required the labour bureau's approval	Enterprise had the authority	Enterprise had the authority
Sources of supply	Graduates from universities and colleges, former military officials/soldiers, previous Party cadres, and managers	Workers recruited before the reform, technical school graduates, former soldiers	Most workers recruited after 1987, technical school graduates, high school graduates, urban labour force	Retired workers, rural labour force

Sources: Interviews and documents held in the enterprises, December 1988–May 1989.

5.3 RECRUITMENT DECISIONS IN 1985 AND 1988

For each of the six enterprises, two recruitment decisions were selected for study, one taken in 1985 and the other in 1988 or 1989 (Table 5.2). In 1985, graduates from universities, colleges and technical schools were the most important source of technical manpower. Therefore the enterprises hoped to recruit as many as possible, but the numbers depended upon the quota allocated by the bureau. Large firms such as Automotive and Audio-Visual enjoyed a special status and could select more university graduates than smaller enterprises such as Pharmaceutical and Electric Switchgear. Audio established its own technical training school and its recruitment in both 1985 and 1988 was from among its own students.

During 1988 and 1989 the introduction of the CRS forced managers to be more selective in recruitment. With a fixed budget for wages/salaries, large firms such as Automotive reduced their recruitment. Two large firms, Audio-Visual and Heavy Electrical, adopted an alternative strategy. Instead of seeking young graduates as employees, they hunted skilled people who had job mobility. Recruitment took place only when a vacancy was identified, whilst the total number of employees was frozen.

Smaller enterprises with more autonomy in recruitment believed that the lack of skilled workers could be solved by selecting more university graduates. Pharmaceutical, for instance, established a research and development institute, which urgently needed university graduates for research. The director instructed the personnel department to contact universities and colleges to select the best candidates.

Actor Involvement and Functions

According to a survey conducted by Wu Zhenkun and his colleagues (1993), personnel management in Beijing is regarded as largely decentralized. Their analysis points out that enterprise managers have the power to decide on recruitment, promotion, training and career development. This finding is consistent with the actor involvement identified in the analysis of the 12 recruitment decisions studied here (Table 5.3).

As can be seen from Table 5.3, the number of recruitment decisions involving the labour authorities – the municipal bureaux of labour and personnel – reduced dramatically from five in 1985 to none in 1988–89, while the involvement of the industrial bureaux reduced

Table 5.2 Recruitment decisions in 1985 and 1988–89

Enterprise	Decisions on recruitment of employees in 1985	Decisions on recruitment of employees in 1988–89
Automotive	Recruitment of 30 college graduates as technicians	Recruitment of 21 university graduates as technicians
Audio-Visual	Selection of 65 trainees from its technical school as operators for a production workshop	Head-hunting and hiring a machine maintenance worker from another factory
Heavy Electrical	Selection of 12 trainees from a bureau's technical school as production workers	Hiring a lorry driver for its transport team
Pharmaceutical	Recruitment of three university graduates for its R&D department	Recruitment of 12 university graduates as technicians
Audio	Selection of 40 trainees from its technical school as technical workers and lathe operators	Selection of 10 trainees from its technical school for its die-making workshop
Electric Switchgear	Selection of one university graduate as a technician	Recruitment of five trainees from a bureau's technical school as machine operators

Source: Interviews held in the enterprises, December 1988, March–September 1989.

Table 5.3 Actors involved and their functions in the 12 recruitment decisions

Actors	Number of decisions involved (N=6) 1985	1988–89	Functions in recruitment decision making
External:			
Municipal labour and personnel bureaux	5	–	In 1985 the bureaux assigned quotas of university/college graduates and approved the recruitment applications of enterprises. After 1988 they only registered newly recruited university/college graduates after the enterprises decided to hire them. Therefore the bureaux were not involved in decisions in 1988 and 1989.
Industrial bureaux	6	4	In 1985, the industrial bureaux transmitted the labour quota from the personnel and labour bureaux to enterprises. In 1988 they provided information on labour supply to the enterprises. For Electric Switchgear they provided supplies of technical school trainees.
Internal:			
Director	6	4	In 1985 directors gave approval before the recruitment application was handed to the bureaux. In 1988 they only approved new recruitment decisions, not those for filling vacancies, such as in Audio-Visual and Heavy Electrical.

continued on page 88

Table 5.3 continued

Actors	Number of decisions involved (N=6)		Functions in recruitment decision making
	1985	*1988–89*	
Deputy directors	6	3	In most cases deputy directors assessed the number of employees required. In Audio-Visual and Heavy Electrical they approved the subsequent decision.
Labour and Personnel departments	6	6	These departments drew up annual recruitment plan, made proposals and selected employees. In 1988 they approved most job changes and filled vacancies, as in the case of Audio-Visual.
Workshop managers	2	4	Workshop managers proposed labour demand plans according to production requirements.
Technical departments	2	2	Technical departments drew up labour demand plans, especially regarding university/college graduates.
Transport department	–	1	In Heavy Electrical, is applied to recruit a driver.
Work group supervisors	–	1	In Audio-Visual, workshop group supervisors applied for a machine maintenance worker.

Source: Interviews held in the enterprises, December 1988, March–September 1989.

from six decisions to four. More importantly, the role of the industrial bureaux had changed, as indicated in the table. They were no longer responsible for approving enterprise recruitment. Rather, their function was to provide information and advice to the enterprises. From 1988 the enterprise managers were fully responsible for recruitment.

With the expansion of enterprise autonomy came some changes in the internal processes. Firstly, the number of decisions involving workshop managers increased from two in 1985 to four in 1988–89. The main personnel function of these production units, as well as the technical departments, was to make their own recruitment proposals. This was strikingly different from the traditional role of operational units, which had passively accepted whoever was allocated to them by the planning authorities. If the allocation of labour in 1985 was a 'top-down' process, recruitment in 1988–89 suggested 'bottom-up' procedures. As one personnel manager at Pharmaceutical said:

> Our function has changed greatly. In the past we persuaded workshop managers to accept workers assigned by the bureaux. Now we meet the needs of our production. As a result the real power for labour decisions now lies in the workshops and departments where the new employees work. Therefore we're in charge of recruitment, not the bureaux.

Secondly, within enterprise management there was a further delegation of responsibility. When recruitment did not increase the number of employees, for instance when a vacancy was filled by head-hunting internally, the decision was handled by functional managers. This was especially evident in Audio-Visual and Heavy Electrical.

Duration and Time Framework

The recruitment decision-making process involved making a plan, so that the time framework covered routine activities such as proposing, assessing and approving. Then personnel managers began the task of selecting the right person from among the candidates. In this research, the duration of recruitment was also studied. Table 5.4 presents the time framework identified in the 12 decisions.

Of the 12 decisions, those dealing with the selection of university graduates in both 1985 and 1988–89 were structured according to university terms. In 1985 the decision-making process started with the

Table 5.4 Duration of the 12 recruitment decisions in 1985 and 1988–89

Enterprises	Duration of the recruitment decisions (weeks)		Main activities and changes
	1985	1988–89	
Automotive	8	10	The main change was that in 1988 the bureau only provided information and assisted the enterprise in selecting university graduates. It took two weeks to make a proposal and another eight weeks to select candidates.
Audio-Visual	12	6	Recruitment in 1985 was a planned process and needed approval from the bureaux. In 1989 it took time to hunt for the right person.
Heavy Electrical	11	10	Recruitment in 1985 was a procedure requiring approval from the bureau. In 1989 a decision was made to seek a suitable driver. It took about 10 weeks to find the best person.
Pharmaceutical	8	10	The director was in charge of both recruitment decisions. In 1988, however, the enterprise did not need the bureaux' approval and selected university graduates according to its own requirements.
Audio	10	10	Both recruitment decisions involved selecting trainees from the enterprise's technical school. These trainees were on a contract basis and their appointment needed no approval from the bureaux. The enterprise drew up a plan and decided the issue.
Electric Switchgear	8	8	The recruitment decision in 1985 was to apply for a university graduate from the personnel bureau's allocation plan. It took time for the approval. In 1988 the enterprise contacted the industrial bureau's technical school for trainees. Most time was spent on negotiating with the schoolmaster and coordinating with the bureau.
Average	9.5	9	

Source: Interviews held in the enterprises, December 1988, March–September 1989.

personnel/labour department drawing up a recruitment plan that was first approved by the director and then authorized by the bureaux. This process usually took two to three months to complete. Then, personnel managers had to wait another two months for candidates to be assigned by the bureau. Therefore the whole procedure could last four or five months.

The six decisions in 1988–89 followed a different process. With the increase in enterprise autonomy, the need for additional recruitment was in most cases decided at the department/workshop level, where operational managers drew up a proposal for staff. This proposal was assessed by the personnel/labour department and approved by the director. Personnel managers also sought information from the industrial bureau, and then made direct contact with universities or colleges supplying graduates. The whole process took only two to three months.

Staff replacement differed from the selection procedure for university graduates. As soon as an employee left a position, workshop managers immediately asked the personnel manager to fill the vacancy. Most time was spent on head-hunting and selecting, which could take about two to three months.

It is interesting to compare the recruitment decisions of two of the enterprises, Automotive and Heavy Electrical. The former relied upon an additional supply of university graduates with high technological skills, while after 1987 the latter only recruited of new employees when there was a vacancy. Their decisions represented typical recruitment procedures in the decentralization programme.

5.4 TOWARDS HUMAN RESOURCE MANAGEMENT: AUTOMOTIVE'S RECRUITMENT

Automotive was established in 1966 following the ministry's decision to establish an automobile production site in Beijing by merging a number of small factories. The enterprise had its own research institute, which carried out new product development as well as technological innovation. In 1984 the enterprise introduced Japanese technology to improve its products and production lines. In 1988 it entered into a joint venture with a Chinese investment company and a Hong Kong partner. The joint venture then decided to invest in a manufacturing site in Beijing. The number of employees rapidly increased from less then 4000 to more than 5000. In 1989, with further expansion, the number of employees reached almost 6100.

In 1985 the enterprise had two personnel departments. One was the labour management department, which took responsibility for manual workers, accounting for more than 72 per cent of total employees. The other was the personnel department in charge of technicians, managers, office clerks and administrative staff, plus the recruitment of university graduates. After 1987 the two departments merged to become the personnel and labour management department. The enterprise's organizational chart in 1989 is shown in Figure 5.1.

Personnel management was within the administration division, whose functions included recruitment, registration, wage rates, welfare issues and performance assessment. Under the central planning system an enterprise was asked to draw up a long-term personnel plan (10 years) and report it to the industrial bureau. The latter then summarized the demand for labour and submitted this to the Municipal Personnel Bureau, which handed over the municipal requirements to the Ministries of Education and Personnel. The ministries and bureaux balanced demand and supply and then assigned graduates to enterprises. Figure 5.2 depicts the formal recruitment procedure in 1985.

The allocation process coordinated by the bureaux was complicated and rigid. The enterprise reported its labour requirements to the industrial bureau, then waited for new employees to be allocated. As the personnel manager of Automotive said:

> In 1985 everything was assigned by the state. Although we had our own personnel development plan, it was always ignored, because the bureau decided how many employees we should have had. As a result, we had no power to decide recruitment and no freedom to choose candidates. We could only accept whoever the bureau sent us.

After 1986 this state control over personnel began to relax. From 1987 the bureaux were no longer responsible for allocating university graduates, and the recruitment was determined by managers. Consequently Automotive switched its emphasis to the development of technical skills. In 1987 technicians with university or college degrees only constituted about 6 per cent of employees. Senior executives felt that the lack of technicians was the main reason for slow technological innovation. The executive committee drew up a human resource development strategy, which required an increase in the number of technicians at the rate of 1 per cent per year. In 1986 the enterprise signed a 10-year agreement with a university in Beijing for a training programme for 400 staff.

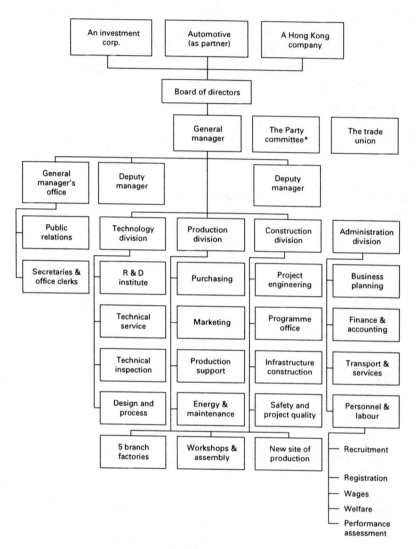

Source: Document held in Automotive, May 1989.

Figure 5.1 Organization Chart of Automotive (joint venture) in 1989

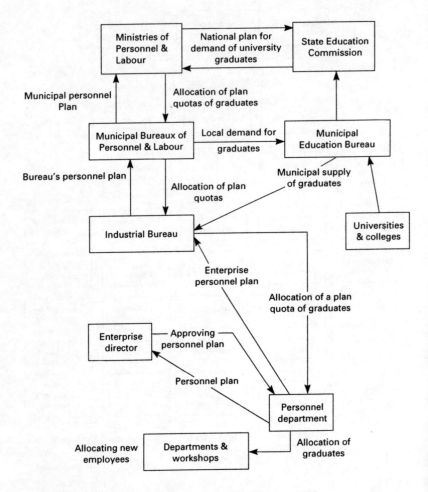

Source: Interviews held in Automotive, March–May 1989.

Figure 5.2   Automative's decision-making process when recruiting
university graduates in 1985

Compared with 1985, by 1989 the enterprise had much more freedom and no plan quota for recruitment and labour management, as Figure 5.3 indicates. Its relationship with the bureau had ended, at least in theory, with the firm's entry into a joint venture, which was governed by a board of directors drawn from the three partners. The industrial bureau no longer had administrative control over the enterprise. According to the personnel manager of Automotive: 'The most progress achieved in recruitment was that we could refuse to accept anyone assigned by the bureau if we didn't need that person. It was impossible before, but now recruitment is according to our needs.'

However, in practice this freedom was challenged. First, the bureau still controlled most of the information regarding the supply of graduates. The selection of new employees relied upon liaison between the enterprise's personnel managers and the bureau. Second, and perhaps more importantly, the enterprise relied upon collaboration with the bureau in other areas such as training, safety checks and quality control. In particular, both the trade union branches and the party remained under the bureau's control. The bureau, on behalf of the government, supervised new product development, technological innovation and investment projects. Despite the transformation from state-owned enterprise to joint venture, it was impossible to cut off all state links. Consequently, the bureau still exerted an influence on the management. The bureau's power can be illustrated by Automotive's recruitment in 1989. The enterprise originally planned to select 20 graduates but it recruited 21, the extra one having been foisted on it by the bureau. Although the candidate had no technical background, the enterprise felt obliged to accept him because he had been introduced by the bureau. As the personnel manager summed it up: 'We have very close relations [with the bureau]. We may [in future] need their help. Although in this case we did not need the bureau's approval, we wanted to keep on good terms with them because there are still a lot of issues that will involve the bureau in future.'

This bargaining relationship between bureaux and enterprises was evident in the recruitment decisions in other enterprises in 1988–89. Pharmaceutical, for instance, attempted not to rely too heavily on the bureau's information on university graduates, but soon found that apart from the bureau there was nowhere else to gather such data. The enterprise finally decided to send personnel to visit some universities in order to establish direct contact with students.

However the relationship with a bureau was critical if it had its own training centres. Electric Switchgear decided to recruit trainees

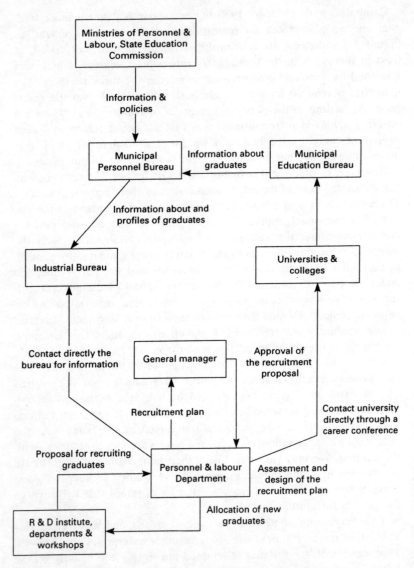

Source: Interviews held in Automotive, May–September 1989.

Figure 5.3   Automative's decision-making process when recruiting
university graduates in 1989

from the bureau's technical school. As highly skilled workers were needed by many firms, trainees were always in a short supply. The allocation of these trainees was strictly controlled by the bureau so the enterprise had to negotiate for an assignment of recruits. In order to obtain good ones, the labour manager of Electric Switchgear used her personal relations (*guanxi*) with the school head to pull off a 'backdoor' deal.

5.5 RECRUITMENT AS A HEAD-HUNTING PROCESS: LOOKING FOR A SPECIALLY SKILLED EMPLOYEE

Through the process of labour reform, employees too gained greater freedom to select jobs they preferred. Job mobility thus became an alternative for the enterprises seeking specially skilled personnel. This approach was mostly used when a vacancy occurred. To some extent this recruitment was harder because the enterprise was faced with the uncertainty of whether or not there would be a sufficient number of applicants with the required skills and whether an applicant was the best for the post. At the same time, the applicants could bargain with the enterprise for specific conditions such as wage rates and fringe benefits, particularly when there was a shortage of skilled workers. Job mobility in China was a complex issue. Chinese enterprises were not only employers, but were obliged to provide welfare, medical care, housing, food, and education for the children of their employees.[6]

Of the 12 recruitment decisions, two in 1988–89 resulted from job vacancies in Audio-Visual and Heavy Electrical. The latter case is examined in detail below.

Heavy Electrical was selected to test the CRS in 1986, one year earlier than other enterprises. The adoption of the CRS and the bureau's relaxation of its control over labour management gave the enterprise sufficient autonomy to determine its recruitment strategy. During 1986 and 1987 the department of personnel and labour conducted a survey of departments and workshops and fixed the number of jobs in each. The survey suggested that at least 20 per cent of its 1800 employees should be made redundant. What the managers did later, which was similar to the findings of Byrd and his colleagues (Byrd, 1992), was to order each department to reduce the number of workers, transferring those who were made redundant to service companies or putting them on an internal training programme. In 1987 the department of personnel and labour introduced a subcontracting system, which froze the wage and salary budget of all departments and workshops. Furthermore the top executives decided to halt recruitment of new employees because they believed that productivity had suffered through redundancy. The enterprise therefore ceased recruiting university graduates and new workers, and turned its attention to head-hunting.

The recruitment of a lorry driver occurred in early 1989. The transport department urgently needed a driver to fill a vacancy. It took about two and a half months to complete the recruitment. Why did it take such a long time to find a lorry driver when the head of the department said that there were many qualified applicants? The delay was due to two factors. The first factor was that the position was not advertised in local newspapers. Nor did the enterprise recruit from the Job Exchange Centre. The labour manager said that they could not trust people from the market because no information was available on their background. What managers were particularly concerned about was an applicant's performance record, behaviour and, more importantly, his/her relations with colleagues. As the labour manager said:

> We seldom contacted the local labour market. As a labour manager I know that well-qualified people do not go there to find a job. Such people are controlled by their organizations and would not be allowed to leave. To leave would need a lot of personal influence [over their managers]. In this case, the reason the driver wanted our position was because he wanted to work in a place closer to his family. More importantly, he was introduced by my friend. We know each other very well, and so I trusted his introduction. From him, I understood the driver was very good.

So personnel searched for the right person through their network of friends and other personal relations (*guanxi*) because 'personal relations are more reliable'. As a result the head-hunting process took time.

The second factor was the difficulty of deciding who was best for the post. The preferences of the enterprise, as an employer, and applicants were never easy to match. In general, an applicant and the labour managers negotiated conditions of employment such as wages and welfare. A new employee was not entitled to apply for housing or accommodation, and the other welfare benefits he or she might be entitled to were the same as those of a contract employee. Some candidates withdrew their application after the negotiations because they did not want to be treated as a contract employee, or they wanted accommodation.

Using friends and personal acquaintances as referees for candidates and presetting conditions to limit a candidate's right to accommodation were evident in the other enterprises. The personnel manager of Audio-Visual asked her colleagues to help her to find a machine maintenance worker. She explained that in this case the concept of 'face' (*mianzi*) was useful: 'If a person is introduced by a friend or relative you trust or know well, it is better for future management control. The referee will later play a role in helping you to supervise the employee's behaviour. In most cases the employee will do well, for the sake of the referee's *mianzi*'.

This informal network built upon personal links was an effective way of transmitting information between enterprises. The labour manager of Audio, for instance, joined an association with other producers to exchange information about the labour supply, which was different from that provided by the bureau. Such news was particularly useful for the enterprise when deciding on training programmes for its technical school.

The underdeveloped housing market became a crucial constraint on the recruitment of employees, who might rely upon the employer to provide accommodation. Pharmaceutical, for instance, limited its selection of graduates from local universities and colleges because it was unable to provide accommodation for them. Large firms were in a better position, but Automotive allocated flats only to those who had been with the company for a long time or who had made a specific contribution. Housing was more attractive to employees than wages and incentives.

5.6 DISCUSSION AND SUMMARY

As China has the largest population in the world, the state put employment at the top of its policy agenda. The traditional approach was to force enterprises to accept as many employees as possible. This policy was largely abandoned after the mid-1980s, when recruitment was handed over to managers, who were instructed to determine the number of employees according to production requirements. Analysis of the 12 recruitment decisions in 1985 and 1988–89 shows that the decentralization programme passed decision-making power to enterprise management, and that all six enterprises enjoyed autonomy in the selection and recruitment of new employees. This finding is consistent with the research of Wu Zhenkun and his colleagues (1992), who noted that personnel management was one of the areas in which enterprise autonomy had increased most. The growth of enterprise freedom of choice followed a change in the function of the bureaux. Both industrial and labour/personnel bureaux relinquished their authority over assigning employees to enterprises, and became providers of information and advice. Furthermore the mobility of workers among the enterprises created another source of labour, as seen in the cases of Audio-Visual and Heavy Electrical.

Recruitment of graduates was planned and fluctuated according to university terms. A significant change in this procedure was that the traditional 'top-down' allocation was replaced by a 'bottom-up' process. Middle managers emerged as the main actors proposing recruitment, whilst directors took part in controlling the size of the workforce.

However the bureaux, as government agencies, remained critical for recruitment because they were the largest source of information. To some extent this limited enterprise autonomy. The recruitment of new employees was often dependent upon the bureau's information supply, in addition to an enterprise's reliance on the bureau's technical trainees. Furthermore the bureau's influence was like a shadow power in many aspects of enterprise activities. As a consequence managers tried to maintain good relations with the bureaux. The rationale for recruitment, as the case of Automotive indicated, was not always driven by economics. It could also reflect social and political factors connected with the bureau.

However, enterprise autonomy in recruitment could be fully realized to fill job vacancies when it came to head-hunting, as suggested by the decisions of Audio-Visual and Heavy Electrical. The analysis of these two decisions indicates that managers preferred social networks such as friendship and personal relations when head-hunting. This attention to non-market mechanisms was a result of the under-developed labour market, where informal links between managers across organizational boundaries became an important channel for circulating information. More importantly, personal relationships were used to build trust between employer and employee. Such use of personal relations (*guanxi*) reflects a Chinese tradition.

Finally, selection has become more difficult because applicants now had some power when negotiating with the enterprises. Apart from her or his wage/salary, an employee had to rely upon the enterprise to provide various benefits. Thus an enterprise with few fringe benefits and limited welfare provisions was less attractive to applicants.

6 Organizational Change: The Relationship between Management and the Communist Party

6.1 ORGANIZATIONAL CHANGE AS A RESPONSE TO THE ENVIRONMENT AND THE MATRIX STRUCTURE IN STATE ENTERPRISES

The purpose of this chapter is to compare the decision-making processes for organizational change in the six enterprises between 1984–86 and 1987–88. Organizational change refers to a wide range of activities that aim to improve organizational performance by means of altering structures, internal relations, procedures and rules. It can also change patterns of behaviour (for example corporate culture and leadership style). Organizational change is usually seen as the organization's response to important changes in the external environment (Pettigrew, 1985b) and internal and external forces stemming from the need to improve interdepartmental coordination and market competitiveness (March, 1981; Whipp et al., 1988).

These day an organization's structure arises as a consequence of its position within the institutional context, which sets the rules, norms and policies (Butler, 1991; Meyer and Rowan, 1977). In China at the time of the study there were two institutional contexts to consider. The first was that of the planning authorities and government agencies such as the administrative and regulatory bureaux. These authorities established a supervisory structure over the enterprises. As described in Chapter 2, there existed a matrix supervisory structure between the enterprises and the bureaux, whereby managers had to report to two bosses, that is, the enterprise director and the staff or executive heading the department in the bureau. This matrix structure was usually called 'corresponding management' (*duikou guanli*). The vertical relationship between departments in the enterprises and bureaux whereby managers were responsible to the government agencies with similar functions was referred to as 'the functional link'. For example in 1985 the MEC ordered all enterprises to establish a total quality control (TQC) office under the direct supervision of the director. It also instructed that an enterprise's TQC office should report directly to the TQC office in the industrial bureau, which was subordinate to the MEC's office.

The second consisted of political organizations under the leadership of the Communist Party. In addition to the governmental administrative structures composed of ministries and bureaux, the Party had an independent organizational structure comprising committees, branches and groups at every level. Thus an enterprise's Party committee reported directly to the bureau's Party committee, which was responsible to the municipal Party committee. The Party was assisted by the National Federation of Trade Unions, which had branches in the bureaux and enterprises.

These two institutional contexts created a complex governance over enterprises, as Figures 2.1 and 2.2 have shown. The rationale for this was that it allowed the government to control and supervise the enterprises efficiently, and ensure that the enterprises were following the Party's political commands. The role of the Party cadre in the enterprises was to control managers and supervise executives' decision making, as well as boosting the morale of employees by non-material means such as praise (*biaoyang*) and honouring worthy examples (*xianjin dianxing*).[1]

State enterprises were also burdened with social obligations, including the provision of social welfare facilities, housing and accommodation for employees, education facilities for employees' children and health care (Li Peilin *et al.*, 1992, pp. 63–6).

As a result the performance of the state enterprises was assessed by a range of criteria that stemmed from their social and political obligations as well as their economic objectives. This gave rise to the phenomenon of 'organized dependency' (Walder, 1986, 1987) and implies that many departments within an enterprise were established for social and political reasons. The situation was worsened by the government policy of 'low salaries and high employment', which led to overmanning. This was described as 'five people doing the work of three' and resulted in poor motivation, low productivity and a lack of discipline.

One objective of the reform in state enterprises was to reduce overmanning and abolish social–political obligations, so as to enable the enterprises to concentrate on increasing productivity. One measure was to introduce the CLS to replace traditional permanent employment. Furthermore, as described in Chapter 5, after the CRS was introduced the government shifted its focus of control from full employment to the wage budget. Some enterprises, such as Audio-Visual and Heavy Electrical, became reluctant to recruit new employees.

While managers gained power in labour recruitment and selection, they were restricted in the number of workers they could lay off. This was because there was no social security system to cope with unemployment. In China, social security and welfare services were provided by the enterprises. As Huang Xiaojing and Yang Xiao (1987, p. 148) note:

China's social security system is actually not 'social' at all. There is no national system covering retirement pensions or medical care. Instead, China's social security system is largely realized by means of employment. Anyone will have welfare benefits and security so long as he or she has a job. . . . The most serious problem in the area of welfare and insurance today is that enterprises have over-spent on workers' retirement pensions and medical care.

In addition to the constraints regarding redundant workers, managers' power to initiate organizational change was limited by their relationship with government agencies in the matrix structure that linked the latter to departments in the enterprises. A change in organizational structure might be considered as disturbing the status quo, prompting intervention by the bureaus. The relationship between Party and management was another sensitive issue. According to the Enterprise Law, the Party was part of the organizational structure, 'guaranteeing and supervising the implementation of the principles and policies adopted by the Party and state in enterprises'. The Party's activities within the enterprise were the responsibility of the Party secretary. The director had no power to decide on issues regarding Party organization, such as how many cadres the enterprise would have. A similar relationship was that between the director and the trade unions.

6.2 ORGANIZATIONAL CHANGE BETWEEN 1984 AND 1986: ESTABLISHMENT OF THE DIRECTOR'S AUTHORITY

Table 6.1 shows examples of organizational change. Six decisions were selected from the period 1984 to 1986, when the DRS was introduced. These decisions mostly concerned the reorganization of relations between departments and changing management systems. From 1984 to 1986 the DRS was widely adopted in enterprises in Beijing and the bureaux handed over more of their powers to directors. For instance

Table 6.1 Organizational changes, 1984–86

Enterprises	Focus of organizational change
Automotive	Reorganization of the labour management system and introduction of a new wage system. The director also replaced the middle management teams.
Audio-Visual	Change in the organizational structure and appointment of new management teams in departments and workshops.
Heavy Electrical	Establishment of three divisions with a new responsibility system. The authority to make decisions was transferred from the Party secretary to the director.
Pharmaceutical	Establishment of a new department of sales and marketing.
Audio	Establishment of a subcontract system in workshops and introduction of a new performance assessment procedure.
Electric Switchgear	Replacement of middle-management teams in departments and workshops.

Sources: Data for Heavy Electrical: interviews and documents, October–December 1986. Data for the other enterprises, interviews and documents, November–December 1988.

the selection and management of middle managers and wage allocation shifted from the bureaux to the directors. The bureaux, following the municipal government's reform policies, encouraged the directors to take more responsibility for the enterprises. For example the Municipal Labour Bureau wanted to try out a new labour management system in Automotive. Thus bureaux instructions became triggers for the director to reorganize relations among departments according to work. Usually organizational change was accomplished by replacing of personnel (c.f. Greiner, 1970), and in the enterprises most directors selected their own managerial teams in order to establish their authority.

Some directors made sweeping changes. At both Heavy Electrical and Audio the directors introduced a subcontracting system that required workshops to be responsible for their own profits and losses, and a new performance assessment system was adopted to link these units' profits to bonuses.

Duration and Time Framework

Organizational change is usually a lengthy process and involves a number of activities. Table 6.2 shows the time framework and main activities involved in the six decisions. As March (1981) notes, ideas that recognize the necessity of change usually set off the process. Regarding the six decisions, this stimulation came from two sources: the bureaux' instructions commanding the directors to follow the DRS programme; and the directors' desire to establish an effective internal control system. The changes at Automotive, Audio-Visual and Electric Switchgear were instigated by the bureaux' instructions, whilst those in the other three were initiated by the directors.

Decision making and change were continuous processes, as Pettigrew (1985b) noted. One activity or action could be a product of previous decisions and a catalyst for subsequent decisions. Executives spent much time discussing and evaluating proposals. Most enterprises formed a steering group, usually headed by the director, which undertook the design of the new organizational chart and the selection of the implementation programme. A design could be assessed and changed several times before the executives made the final choice.

These organizational changes were often given a political slant. Many enterprises organized political training programmes to encourage consensus among managers and employees, who were told that the reforms followed state policies. Political slogans, such as 'separating the government from enterprises' (*zhengqi fenkai*) and 'separating the Party from management' (*dangzheng fenkai*), were displayed on wall posters (*qiang bao*) around buildings and workshops. All managers and workers were required to support the changes.

Actor Involvement and Functions

A necessary condition for organizational change was the support of the top leadership (Greiner, 1970), especially when changes affected relations between departments or replaced middle-level managers. Therefore leadership involvement was needed, and the level of decision making was usually centralized. This was observed in the six decisions.

Table 6.3 shows that many actors, internal and external, were involved. External actors included the industrial and functional bureaux. The industrial bureaux participated in three decisions at Automotive, Audio-Visual and Electric Switchgear by issuing instructions and participating

Table 6.2 Duration and time framework of decision-making processes in organizational changes 1984 and 1986

Enterprise	Duration from proposal to approval (weeks)	Decisions/activities
Automotive	21	The department of enterprise management organized a training programme for all middle managers during the first three weeks. It took more than 10 weeks to design and select an appropriate wage system. The rest of the time was spent on discussions among the executives. The Workers' Congress quickly approved the programme at its annual conference.
Audio-Visual	26	The first eight weeks were devoted to education and training (all middle managers and workgroup supervisors). It took almost 15 weeks for design, selection and executive approval. It took another three weeks to gain the bureau's permission.
Heavy Electrical	14	Design and training took place at the same time, taking more than 12 weeks. The director and executives gave final approval in two weeks.
Pharmaceutical	11	The first design took four weeks, then it was revised. At the same time a training programme was organized for middle managers. It took another seven weeks to finish the second design and obtain final approval.
Audio	13	The first four weeks were spent training middle managers. At the same time the management department started its design, taking four weeks. Most time was spent on discussions between directors and the Party secretary, assessing and changing the design.
Electric Switchgear	13	The first two weeks were absorbed by a training programme for the middle managers. Most time was spent discussing the responsibility system for workshops. It took almost eight weeks to finish the final design.
Average	16.3	

Sources: Data for Heavy Electrical: interviews and documents, October–December 1986. Data for the other enterprises: interviews and documents, November–December 1988.

Table 6.3 Actors involved and their function in organizational changes, 1984 and 1986

Name of actor	Number of decisions (N = 6)	Functions of actor in decision making
External: Industrial bureau	3	The bureaux gave direct instructions to two large firms – Automotive and Audio-Visual – and examined and approved the changes. In Electric Switchgear, the bureau ordered the changes.
Municipal Labour Bureau	1	For Automotive only, it helped to establish a new wage–budget system and approved the system.
Experts from a university	1	For Automotive only, a team was assigned by the Labour Bureau to design the wage–budget system and conduct a survey among workers.
Internal: Workers' Congress	1	For Automotive only, the Congress agreed with the director's programme of change.
Director	6	Approved the organizational design and the appointment of middle managers. The directors also led a steering group to design structures, regulations and responsibility systems.
Party secretary	5	At all but Heavy Electrical the Party secretaries participated in the assessment of the design and coordinated with the director to select personnel as candidates for middle management.
Deputy directors	6	Mostly in design and assessment, under the director's instruction.
Trade union chairperson	2	Only at Automotive and Audio-Visual, participating in the assessment procedures.
Enterprise management department	6	Organizing training programmes and designing organizational structure, new responsibility systems and performance assessment measures.
Departments of labour and personnel	6	Designing labour management responsibilities and performance assessment measures.
Other departments (finance)	1	At Automotive, the changes required to introduce a new wage–budget system. The finance manager provided information and was trained to use the new system.

Sources: Data for Heavy Electrical, interviews and documents, October–December 1986. Data for the other enterprises, interviews and documents, November–December 1988.

in selection and approval. For instance at Audio-Visual the bureau appointed the Party secretary as director. This new director then changed the overall structure and appointed all the middle managers. The situation in Electric Switchgear was slightly different in that the director was not a Party member, and this limited his decision-making powers because the Party secretary actually dominated. The bureau then replaced the Party secretary and directed the changes. The situation in Automotive was more complicated. As it had been selected by the municipal government to test a new wage scheme, the changes were closely supervised by the Municipal Labour Bureau, which introduced a team of experts from a university to design the enterprise's wage system and performance assessment measures.

In the remaining decisions the bureaux also played a crucial role in organizing political training, arranging for managers to visit model factories and conveying state policies and documents to the enterprises. The most important role of the bureaux was to implement the DRS and then reshape the relationship between the director and the Party secretary. In all the enterprises the bureaux replaced the directors and/ or the Party secretaries before or after the changes started[2] in order to counteract conflict and resistance from the political staff. The new directors were selected because of their knowledge of production and technology, and their reliable political records and working histories. This gave the directors more clout than previously.

In spite of the official policy that emphasized the importance of the Workers' Congress, neither it nor the trade unions played any role in the decisions made between 1984 and 1986. Organizational change was regarded as an administrative issue not affecting workers, and many believed that such changes did not need the consent of the Workers' Congress. The exception was Automotive, where a new wage system was proposed and winning over workers was seen as important. Therefore the proposals were discussed at a Congress meeting, and representatives approved the changes.

Of the internal actors, two departments were crucial in designing and planning the changes. The enterprise management department undertook tasks such as drafting regulations, drawing up a new organization chart, determining relations among departments and organizing political education programmes within the enterprises. Personnel managers helped the director to select candidates and in some cases ordered middle managers to introduce performance assessments. The influence of other departments, for example finance, was limited. Their input was the provision of information.

Characteristics of Organizational Change from 1984 to 1986

The aim of the changes was twofold. One was to modify the relationship between directors and Party secretaries, giving directors decision-making powers. The other was to establish an effective and efficient administrative hierarchy under the director. Both were only partially achieved. The Party secretary's power over management was reduced, but the director was still constrained by the Party committee. In spite of the fact that the DRS gave the director full authority to decide on organizational structure and personnel, in practice strategic decisions were taken collectively within the Party committee. The directors of Audio-Visual and Electric Switchgear said that their management system was actually the 'director's responsibility under the Party committee's leadership' (*dangwei lingdao xia de changzhang fuze zhi*). Even in enterprises where the directors were dominant, such as at Heavy Electrical, important issues still needed the approval of the party committee.

This shows that the changes did not affect Party organizations. Giving power to directors was not viewed as a challenge to the Party. In fact most directors, except the one at Electric Switchgear, were also members of the Party committee. Their professional position was inseparable from their political status. As a manager of Audio said:

> In theory, we have separated the Party from management with the executive committee, the Party committee and the managerial committee. In reality many of the committee members are the same people. For example the director is also the deputy secretary of the Party committee, and the Party secretary is a member of the executive committee. As a result many decisions, especially strategic ones, are taken collectively by the same people as before.

As a result the changes between 1984 and 1986 were limited to administration.

Bureaux intervention was evident, too. As the matrix structure required direct links between enterprises and bureau departments, any changes in organizational structure disturbed these. At Heavy Electrical, for instance, the director decided to remove most of the technical department from the headquarters building to workshops. As a result a number of technicians involved in product design and production processes were allocated to production lines, avoiding bureaucratic procedures between the department and workshops. Once this had been accomplished the bureau's technical department found it difficult to communicate with the technicians, and the bureau eventually requested that the technicians be returned to the headquarters. Most managers lacked experience in organizational change. Two enterprises, Pharmaceutical and Electric Switchgear, had never had organizational charts before. At Heavy Electrical and Audio the directors quickly shifted all workshops into independent profit centres. This increase of autonomy at the workshop level created some chaos. Workshop managers refused to accept production tasks assigned from departments, but engaged in other business activities to make money. The directors then had to recentralize all decision-making powers and take over control.

6.3   ORGANIZATIONAL CHANGE IN 1987 AND 1988 THROUGH GOVERNMENT INTERVENTION

In 1988 the Beijing municipal government launched an official scheme aimed at improving labour productivity in state enterprises. The municipal government introduced a set of policies known as the RLO (rationalizing labour organizations). This set off changes in the organizational structure of most of the enterprises.

The scheme was initiated by the MEC. The commission conducted a survey in a number of enterprises and found that labour productivity was disappointing. After the adoption of the CRS in 1986 and 1987 the government expected managers to implement the CLS and improve labour productivity by means of introducing labour contracts. In reality most workers and staff remained in permanent employment. Overmanning, low productivity, waste of human resources and low technical skills were the main problems, not only in state enterprises but also in joint ventures. On the evidence of the survey, the MEC suggested that enterprises be forced to reduce redundancy and that all life-long jobs be transformed into contract-based ones. This proposal was accepted by the municipal government and was called 'rationalizing labour organizations' (RLO – *you hua laodong zuhe*).

This was an official campaign with a 'politicization process' – a term used by Riskin (1987)[3] to describe social change in China. It was a 'top-down' process. When the municipal government decided to launch the scheme, 97 senior officials from 16 industrial and commercial bureaux were assigned to 119 enterprises to implement it (Beijing MEC, 1988). Each bureau drew up a timetable, then assigned a number of working teams to the enterprises to supervise the changes. The targets set by the MEC were to reduce the total workforce by 10 per cent by the end of 1988 and 30 per cent by the end of 1990. The MEC also stipulated that by 1992 all employees in the enterprises should have signed labour contracts.

The municipal government instigated political training programmes to impose the changes on the enterprises. From 15–17 July 1988 the municipal government conducted a three-day conference for senior officials of the bureaux and large enterprises. During the conference, representatives from model factories – enterprises testing the CLS as a pilot group – presented their experiences, then the municipal mayor, Chen Xitong, made a speech asking all officials, managers, party cadres and workers to support the scheme (Chen Xitong, 1988). The MEC organized five workshops to train personnel and labour managers. Industrial bureaux organized a total of 59 training programmes, involving 4270 enterprise managers.[4] These managers later organized political education programmes within their enterprises to train lower-level managers and employees.

The media proclaimed the changes with political slogans. From June to August 1987 the *Beijing Daily*, the municipal government's newspaper, published nine editorial comments on the RLO and reported progress in the model factories. The scheme was labelled 'a breakthrough in the reform' (*Beijing Daily*, 14 August 1988). Permanent employment was described as an 'iron, bowl' (*tie fanwan* – an employee had a job for life), the personnel system as an 'iron chair' (*tie jiaoyi* – a manager always stayed in office) and the wage system as 'iron wages' (*tie gongzi* – wages were guaranteed by the government). The changes were aimed at 'smashing these three irons into pieces', implying that all employees would have contract-based employment and their wages would be determined by performance assessment. Any hesitation or delay in implementing the changes was criticized as 'attempting to halt the reforms'. Thus the scheme became compulsory and required everyone's total acceptance.

Under such pressure the pace of implementation accelerated rapidly. When the scheme was officially announced in July 1988 only 44 enterprises were working within the CLS. By the October this figure had shot up to 770, involving 366 000 employees. In early 1989 it was reported that another 1738 enterprises were participating, accounting for another 780 000 employees. A short while later 1542 enterprises were reported to have completed the implementation process.[5]

The reality differed significantly from the official picture, and there were many problems. The RLO policy created a contradictory situation: it forced the enterprises to remove redundant workers from workshop production positions, while at the same time the municipal government insisted that redundant workers should remain in the enterprises because there were no social security facilities to deal with unemployment. Managers were expected to provide new job opportunities. The municipal government permitted the enterprises to open service companies to absorb the redundant workers. However it found later that many enterprises had placed these workers in internal training programmes and then taken them back to the workshops. Those who were permanently removed were workers close to retirement or with a history of illness.

Many workers felt betrayed and frustrated because they had been educated to believe that life-long employment was one advantage of socialism, whilst unemployment was the result of capitalism.[6] Their resistance made many managers unwilling to carry out the scheme as they wanted to avoid confrontations with their employees. They implemented the scheme in a half-hearted manner rather than taking it seriously.

However the adoption of the CRS and the municipal governmental scheme in 1988 did stimulate organizational change in the enterprises. Six decisions, aimed at reorganizing labour management during the period 1987–88, were selected for the purpose of this research (Table 6.4). Automotive's decision to enter into a joint venture took place in 1987 – the director decided to select suitable employees for the new manufacturing sites. The other five decisions were a result of the RLO, with a reduction in the number of employees as their main aim.

Duration and Time Framework

One characteristic of these organizational changes under the RLO scheme was that their activities were set by the municipal government. This can be identified by comparing enterprise and municipal government schedules (Table 6.5). The decision making and changes in the five enterprises were structured according to the bureaux' wishes. Drawing up the structural changes and labour contracts, selecting appropriate programmes and training managers and workers was a lengthy process. Table 6.6 shows the main activities and the length of time involved in the decision-making process.

Table 6.6 indicates that the changes were complex. Some activities, such as design and assessment, were repeated until a satisfactory

Table 6.4 Organizational change, 1987 and 1988

Enterprise	Focus of organizational change
Automotive	Introduction of the CLS and reorganization of the structure. This resulted in the creation of four subsidiary factories and the introduction of a new performance assessment system.
Audio-Visual	Redesign of the organizational chart. This was to dissolve the department of education and to establish a corporate culture department under the Party secretary. It also established an internal labour market, providing services to redundant workers.
Heavy Electrical	Elimination of the education department and a reduction of redundant workers. It set up an internal labour market with the bureau to mobilize workers.
Pharmaceutical	Creation of two new workshops and introduction of the CLS under the municipal government's instruction. It also rearranged the relationship between departments and appointed the Party secretary as deputy director of production.
Audio	Elimination of seven departments and introduction of the CLS. It split workshops into small business units responsible for their own profits and losses.
Electric Switchgear	Elimination of three departments and introduction of the CLS. It also reduced the number of employees and established an exchange relationship with a service company to supply redundant workers.

Sources: Interviews and documents, November–December 1988.

Table 6.5 Government activities in the RLO scheme and time framework of organizational change in the enterprises, 1987 and 1988

Date	Government activities	Decision activities within the enterprises
1987 March–September	Adoption of the CRS. The Ministry of Labour and Personnel promoted the reform in labour management and organized experiments in some enterprises with the CLS.	Automotive started to design a new organizational structure for the joint venture. In July it conducted a work study in production workshops and found that the average working time was only 4.6 out of eight hours. The director decided to establish a steering group to design a new labour management system for the joint venture.
October–December	The MEC started its investigation of labour productivity under the CRS.	Automotive assessed three alternative designs. The final one included a new organizational chart, contract-based employment, a performance assessment system and a set of regulations and policies regarding responsibilities and rewards. The proposal provoked intensive debate among representatives of the Workers' Congress.
1988 January–March	The MEC conducted a field study in a number of enterprises and found that the average working time in state enterprises was 3.2 out of eight hours. It drafted a report to propose a productivity drive.	Automotive started to implement its new organizational structure. Managers and workers were asked to sign an annual contract. The directors of Audio-Visual and Heavy Electrical participated in a working conference organized by the MEC. At the conference they were informed of the MEC's investigation. They were also asked by the bureaux to prepare for the labour reform.

April and May	The MEC organized a working conference, at which enterprise directors were informed of the labour reform policies. Representatives of model factories gave briefings on their methods and experiences. 16 industrial bureaux started training programmes for enterprise managers and selected large enterprises, including Audio-Visual and Heavy Electrical, to prepare for the CLS.	Automotive completed its labour contract and became a joint venture. Audio-Visual and Heavy Electrical started organizing training programmes for middle managers. Their personnel and labour managers worked with staff from the bureaux to design a contract system. Audio-Visual revised its design following the bureau's instruction to establish an internal labour market. Pharmaceutical and Audio participated in the bureaux' training programmes regarding the future labour reform and respective policies.
June and July	The scheme was formally called 'Rationalizing labour organization' (RLO) by the municipal government. The MEC set targets and schedules for industrial bureaux to complete the scheme. Industrial bureaux continued training programmes and circulated internal documents, including government policies, regulations and instructions for the future programme. Staff from the bureau worked closely with enterprise managers to implement the scheme.	The enterprises were grouped according to the MEC's schedule. The enterprises established a steering group, consisting of the director, the Party secretary, the trade union chairperson, one deputy director and managers in the personnel and labour departments, except for Electric Switchgear, which was asked to start the scheme in September. Most middle managers were given political education training. Personnel and labour managers visited model factories to learn from their experiences. Heavy Electrical finished its organizational design. Pharmaceutical established a pilot programme to reform its research institute.

continued on page 116

Table 6.5 continued

Date	Government activities	Decision activities within the enterprises
August and September	The municipal government published its regulation to protect the directors and managers in the scheme. The MEC urged that the progress of the RLO be accelerated.	Both Audio-Visual and Heavy Electrical finished their revised designs and handed them to their Workers' Congress. Audio-Visual's Party secretary led a pilot programme in the education department. Pharmaceutical and Audio finished their designs. Audio started a pilot programme in the purchasing department and inventory warehouses. Electric Switchgear began training managers.
October	10 functional bureaux jointly published a policy to permit enterprises to open various businesses as a way of employing redundant workers.	Audio-Visual finished its pilot study and started implementation of the CLS. Heavy Electrical chose its training centre to test the labour contract. Pharmaceutical and Audio decided to implement the change. Electric Switchgear started its design
November and December	The MEC assessed progress and required industrial bureaux to finish the scheme. The Labour Bureau reported its summary to the municipal government.	The enterprises were implementing the changes, except Electric Switchgear, which was assessing its design. In late December the director of Electric Switchgear approved the design and decided to introduce the CLS.
1989 January to March	The MEC set a new target for the second stage of the scheme to further the CLS. The scheme was later interrupted by the pro-democracy upheaval from April to June in Beijing.	In January Electric Switchgear started implementing the change and reported its completion in February. The rest of the enterprises reported to the bureaux that they had achieved the targets set by the government.

Sources: Interviews and documents held in the enterprises and the MEC, January–May and July–August 1989.

Table 6.6 Duration of the decision-making processes regarding organizational change 1987 and 1988

Enterprise	Duration from initiation to approval (weeks)	Decision activities
Automotive	42	It took almost 10 weeks to design the work study measures, plus 12 weeks to conduct the study in all departments and workshops, and six weeks to select the design. The final proposal was circulated among the Workers' Congress representatives and discussed for another 10 weeks.
Audio-Visual	35	The decision involved two weeks of internal discussion among executives. The first design of the organizational structure took four weeks, then had to be revised. It took almost 15 weeks to work with the bureau to finish the design. At the same time, the training programme started. It took another six weeks to test the labour contract in a pilot study and four weeks to assess the result. Final approval was given by the Workers' Congress after four weeks of discussions.
Heavy Electrical	30	It took 16 weeks to train managers, design and select the organizational structure. It took another four weeks to coordinate with the bureau for the issue of an internal labour market, and four weeks to discuss at the Workers' Congress. It took four weeks to complete the pilot programme. Then the director exchanged opinions with other executives and approved the change in other departments.
Pharmaceutical	21	It took 15 weeks to finish the organizational design and training programme. At that time it also tested the labour contract in its research institute. Then the director and executives took about six weeks to discuss and approve the changes.
Audio	18	It took 13 weeks for managers to learn from other factories and design their own system. The contract system was first tested in one department. The remaining five weeks was for an assessment of the test, revision of the design and approval.
Electric Switchgear	16	It took four weeks to train managers. Then the programme was stopped because of production pressure. Designing started again after six weeks. It took four weeks for further discussion among the executives. Then the bureau urged that the process be speeded up. It took two weeks to approve the contract system.
Average time	27	

Source: Interviews held in the enterprises, November–December 1988, January–May and July–August 1989.

alternative was found. The time taken for decisions over RLO implementation was almost double that of the changes in 1984 and 1986, the average being about 27 weeks. The processes embraced certain normal activities such as (1) training programmes organized by the municipal government, the bureaux and the enterprises, in which managers and staff were briefed on policies, regulations and instructions; (2) establishing a steering group in charge of organizational design; (3) assessing various proposals for changes; and (4) a pilot programme to test the labour contract and provide feedback to the director, prior to approving the proposed changes.

The bureaux played a crucial role in organizing and supervising the process. At the same time, as the changes affected workers' interests, the support of the top executives was needed to implement the new labour management system. All this led to the involvement of a number actors in the process (Table 6.7).

Table 6.7 shows that there was no involvement of the functional bureaux, such as the municipal personnel and labour bureaux. But the number of decisions in which the industrial bureaux participated increased from three to five, compared with those shown in Table 6.3. The industrial bureaux were particularly concerned with large firms. For instance, Audio-Visual's first proposal was rejected by the bureau, which asked the managers to redesign the enterprise's organizational structure and establish an internal labour market. At Heavy Electrical the personnel and labour managers worked closely with the bureau to exchange its workers with those of other enterprises.

Table 6.7 also shows that the Workers' Congress participated in the three decisions by Automotive, Audio-Visual and Heavy Electrical, but as Table 6.3 has shown, it previously participated only in Automotive's case. This suggests that the role of the Congress in the large enterprises had become more important, and indeed the Congress gave the final approval for changes in these firms.

However there remains the question of whether the Congress had real power or whether it was merely a rubber stamp, because it was the directors who decided whether or not it should be involved. The directors of Automotive, Audio-Visual and Heavy Electrical said that they thought it was necessary to obtain Congress' consent because the RLO changed the wage system, affecting workers' interests. The directors required Congress representatives to persuade redundant workers to leave. The directors of the other enterprises thought otherwise, believing it was not necessary to have Congress' approval because the changes were being enforced by the municipal government. Therefore,

Table 6.7 Actors involved and their functions in the organizational changes, 1987 and 1988

Actor	Number of decisions involved (N = 6)	Functions of actors in decision making
External:		
Industrial bureaux	5	Initiating the changes according to the MEC's schedule. In Audio-Visual and Heavy Electrical they also participated in design and selection activities, and approved Audio-Visual's design.
Internal:		
Workers' Congress	3	In Automotive, Audio-Visual and Heavy Electrical: approval of the new labour management system.
Director	6	Leading a steering group and participating in design and selection, and in some cases approving the design before the Workers' Congress. Ultimate approval in Pharmaceutical, Audio and Electric Switchgear.
The Party secretary	5	Except Automotive, where there was no Party secretary from late 1987 to early 1989. Mostly involved in selecting an organizational design, consulting with the director for approval. In Audio-Visual the Party secretary organized the pilot programme.
Deputy directors	6	Mostly in design and selection of new systems regarding labour management.
Trade union chairperson	6	Participation in selection, as a member of the steering group, and in some cases coordinating with the Workers' Congress in the approval procedure.
Enterprise management department	6	Organizing political training programmes, designing new systems and drafting responsibility regulations for departments and workshops.
Departments of labour and personnel	6	Coordinating with the bureaux to collect information and to circulate internal policies on labour management, providing information for the directors regarding personnel and drafting labour contracts for managers and workers.

Sources: Interviews and documents held in the enterprises, November–December 1988, January–May and July–August 1989.

whether or not the Congress agreed, the enterprises had to implement the changes.

Although the directors had different opinions on the Congress, all agreed that the trade unions should be consulted and involved, because the union representatives could act as intermediaries between management and workers. The unions had only a limited contribution to make, participating in the selection of the programmes but having little influence on the outcome.

As the changes resulted from a 'top-down' process, only two departments – management, and personnel and labour – participated in the decision making. As in the earlier period, they were mainly responsible for training, coordinating with the bureaux and designing management systems, as well as drafting department responsibilities and labour contracts.

6.4 THE PROGRESS AND PROBLEMS OF ORGANIZATIONAL CHANGE UNDER THE RLO SCHEME

The RLO scheme in 1988 and the DRS from 1984 to 1986 had some similarities. As municipal government reform programmes, both had 'top-down' intervention and were politicized with ideological slogans and political training programmes. But the bureaux participated more in the RLO. As a result of government enforcement, the enterprises had to achieve the targets set by the MEC. By the end of 1988 all the enterprises but Automotive reported that they had reduced employment by 10 per cent. In January 1989 the MEC announced the second phase of the RLO, aimed at reducing employment in state industries by 30 per cent. This, however, was interrupted by the pro-democracy upheavals in Beijing from April to June 1989.

The RLO raised many questions regarding improved labour productivity. The decision-making and implementation processes within the enterprises took longer and were more complex than before. Key factors influencing the changes were relations between the enterprises and bureaux and those between the directors and the Party secretaries. Moreover, imperfect social security systems compounded the difficulty of implementing the RLO.

The Intervention of the Bureaux

Compared with 1985, in 1988 the power of the industrial bureaux to control the enterprises had reduced, largely because adoption of the CRS meant that the bureaux had to separate themselves from enterprise management. Most decisions concerning personnel and labour management were now delegated to the directors. Furthermore, after 1987 the directors had more power to determine wages and rewards.

However the bureaux retained a critical position as administrative authorities, and directors and Party secretaries were appointed by the bureaux. Strategic decisions such as investment also required their approval (for further details, see Chapter 7). The bureaux acted on behalf of the state, forcing the enterprises to accept the government's orders and policies. The latter role was seen particularly in the acceptance of the RLO scheme. As a senior official in the Municipal Electronics Industrial Office, the bureau in charge of Audio-Visual and Audio, said, the bureau had become an intermediary between the municipal government and the enterprises. Administrative intervention was seen as an important tool in improving enterprise management. As he put it:

We are seriously concerned that enterprise directors may neglect management once they have signed a profit contract. For managers, it is much easier to make a profit by increasing prices or having poor quality outputs. So it is necessary to put some pressure on them to improve the quality of their management.

It was not surprising to find that it was the municipal government, rather than the enterprises, that set the objectives for the changes. As an official of the MEC said:

We made a policy, the 5-5-1, to implement the RLO scheme. This means that during the first phase 50 per cent of enterprises and 50 per cent of employees should be involved, and 10 per cent of workers should be removed from the enterprises. Our administrative tools were the industrial bureaux. Through the bureaux, we could implement the scheme and improve enterprise management.

Different managers responded differently to bureau intervention in the RLO scheme. The directors of Audio-Visual, Pharmaceutical and Audio supported the RLO scheme and emphasized that bureau intervention was helping them to remove redundant workers from production lines. The other directors believed that although the scheme was important, they were unhappy with orders being dictated by the municipal government. They wanted to see a state social security system in place prior to labour rationalization, otherwise it would be almost impossible to implement the RLO scheme.

In addition to direct intervention by the bureaux, the matrix structure linked the enterprises to the bureaux. The relationship between departments in the enterprises and their counterparts in the bureaux made change difficult. The matrix relationship between departments in Audio-Visual and the bureau before and after the changes are shown in Figure 6.1. As can be seen the changes brought by the RLO meant the merging of some departments and the creation of a legal section. This structure permitted the movement of internal documents, regulations, decision approval and state policies from the bureaux to the enterprises.

The RLO did not reduce the welfare obligations of enterprises. Managers retained their excess workers to cope with future demands, most of which were imposed by the municipal government. For instance the director of Heavy Electrical said that he had had to dispatch a team of workers for traffic duty on the road in front of the enterprise following an order from the municipal government's traffic security committee. A survey at Audio-Visual found that in the first half of 1989 it received 242 internal documents and instructions from different authorities.[7] About 20 concerned employee welfare and medical care. In 1988 the enterprise received 343 internal documents, 26 of which dealt with welfare issues. This shows welfare is an important area of concern. [8]

Party Secretaries with Administrative Positions

Redundant labour, according to the official definition, included workers and staff who made no direct contribution to production. Thus full-time political staff working for the Party and the trade unions fell into this category. While the RLO did not openly encourage the shedding of political staff, in practice they were removed. Table 6.8 compares the number of political staff before and after the RLO was introduced. As Table 6.8 indicates, the number of Party cadres and offices of Party organizations reduced considerably. Moreover the enterprises started to introduce new personnel policies as promotion criteria emphasizing managers' track records rather than their political attitudes. In all six

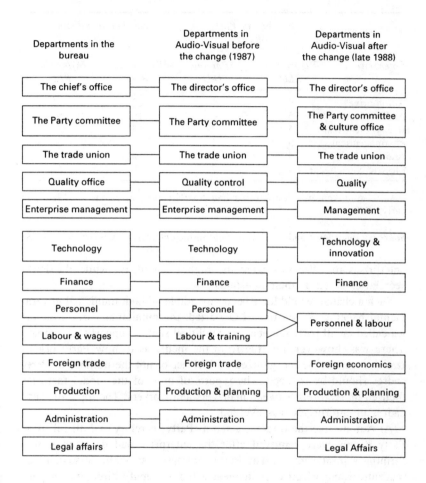

Departments in the bureau	Departments in Audio-Visual before the change (1987)	Departments in Audio-Visual after the change (late 1988)
The chief's office	The director's office	The director's office
The Party committee	The Party committee	The Party committee & culture office
The trade union	The trade union	The trade union
Quality office	Quality control	Quality
Enterprise management	Enterprise management	Management
Technology	Technology	Technology & innovation
Finance	Finance	Finance
Personnel	Personnel	Personnel & labour
Labour & wages	Labour & training	
Foreign trade	Foreign trade	Foreign economics
Production	Production & planning	Production & planning
Administration	Administration	Administration
Legal affairs		Legal Affairs

Source: Documents in Audio-Visual, November–December 1988, March 1989.

Figure 6.1 Matrix relationship between departments in Audio-Visual and its bureau before and after the RLO

Table 6.8   Number of Party offices and full-time Party cadres before and
after the RLO in 1988

	Number of Party offices		Number of full-time cadres	
Enterprise	Before the RLO	After the RLO	Before the RLO	After the RLO
Automotive*	9	–	22	–
Audio-Visual	5	2	10	5
Heavy Electrical	5	2	15	8
Pharmaceutical	5	1	8	5
Audio	4	1	8	4
Electric Switchgear	4	2	9	5

* As a joint venture, Automotive had no Party organizations in 1988 and
early 1989.

Sources: Interviews and documents held in the enterprises, January–May 1989.

enterprises the directors were the highest authority, while the Party
secretaries acted as their assistants.

Such a change would have been impossible without municipal governmental backing. When the RLO started, the municipal Party committee called on all party members and political staff to support the scheme.[9]
There was, however, no clue from the media as to how Party organizations were to be reorganized or whether or not the number of Party
cadres should be reduced. The reports of most of the model factories
focused on relations between managers and workers. The topic of Party
cadres in enterprises was avoided.

At Automotive the director acted as Party secretary and all full time
Party cadres were removed after the enterprise had declared it was
forming a joint venture. The Party secretaries at Audio-Visual, Pharmaceutical and Electric Switchgear acted as deputy directors for general administration and production. They said they should also understand
production and the Party's task was thus part of the enterprise business. At Heavy Electrical and Audio, Party secretaries were not part
of the administrative system. The Party offices had few political tasks,
mainly publishing newsletters and undertaking technical training and
political education.

In all six enterprises, no conflict between the directors and the party
secretaries was reported – the directors had established their authority.
The DRS had offered directors an opportunity to select their own

managerial teams, consisting of executives and middle managers reporting directly to the director rather than the Party secretary. Directors had thus formed their own coalitions. Compared with Party secretaries, directors knew more about production and technology, and had worked in the enterprises for many years.

The CRS made the director the legal representative of the enterprise in contractual matters. It also shifted the emphasis on political attitudes and loyalty to economic criteria such as profitability. This made managers and workers more concerned with business activities and production tasks. Thus material benefits became the main incentives for employees, while non-material rewards, such as political approval, quickly declined in attraction. This weakened the authority of the Party cadres, who had controlled employees through political incentives.

In the majority of enterprises, most strategic decisions were taken by the executive committee. Although the Party secretaries participated in these meetings, it was evident that their status was below that of the directors. This situation lasted until June 1989, when the army crushed the pro-democracy movement in Tiananmen square. The enterprises in Beijing were ordered to reinstate the powers of the Party secretaries. At Automotive, for instance, a new Party secretary was appointed by the bureau. In the other enterprises the Party secretaries were instructed to concentrate on political tasks and take more responsibility for personnel management. However it was evident that it was becoming increasingly difficult for the Party to retain control of the enterprises. As a result of the progress of decentralization, the director's authority had been firmly established.

Difficulties and Problems with the RLO

In general, managers were cautious about laying off redundant workers, partly to avoid a confrontation with workers. Although the directors wanted to improve productivity, the middle managers were usually hesitant to take action. Thus three main factors acted to impede the progress of the RLO.

First, as stated before, in spite of the MEC's order to reduce employees by 10 per cent, the municipal government told the enterprises to provide job opportunities for redundant workers. The enterprises established various companies, most of which contracted with the enterprises to share material supplies, transportation, cleaning, packaging and trading. Some companies opened restaurants and hotels. Electric Switchgear established a cleaning company to serve a joint-venture hotel, and this helped the enterprise dispose of more than 80 workers. Second, enterprises had to provide their employees with welfare benefits. Therefore it was impossible to sever relations completely between the enterprise and employees. For instance many employees lived in enterprise accommodation. If they left, they would have to give up their flats or houses. As one executive in Audio said:

> We indeed wanted some workers to leave, because they were lazy or unskilled. But we couldn't get rid of them, because they were in our flats. If they were to leave the enterprise, they would have to vacate the flats. But they were unable to give them up to find other accommodation, so we had to keep them on.

Third, many managers did not like to cause friction. Workers who were removed from production positions felt they had suffered a loss of face (*mianzi*), a concept that implied public humiliation. Therefore workshop managers, who worked closely with the workers, were generally unwilling to lay them off.

Although some redundant workers were transferred to service companies, many stayed within the enterprises waiting to be assigned to workshops. By the end of 1988 the five enterprises reported to the MEC that they had completed the RLO and reduced their production employees by 10 per cent. But a closer inspection of the figures revealed another picture. For instance, Audio reported that it had laid off 171 workers. Of these, 30 (17.5 per cent) had transferred to Audio's service companies, 40 (23.4 per cent) had been due to retire or had a long history of illness, 16 (9 per cent) had resigned, and only nine (5.3 per cent) had been dismissed. The remaining 76 were given training and then returned to their workshops. At Audio-Visual, where more than 300 workers were said to have left, 170 had remained in the internal labour force and participated in training programmes. Later, 121 returned to the workshops. The rest were dispatched to service companies or retired. Pharmaceutical reported it had removed 103 employees. Of these, 24 had been due to retire or suffered from long-term illness, 27 were dispatched to service companies and seven resigned. The remaining 55 had participated in training programmes and/or had been dispatched to start a branch factory, returning to the workshops after they had completed their training and their project. The achievements of the RLO were thus largely discounted, since many redundant workers later returned to their previous positions.

More seriously, although all employees in the enterprises signed one-or two-year labour contracts, only newly recruited junior workers were bound by these contracts, while employees recruited before 1987 still enjoyed permanent employment. Therefore implementation of the CLS was a slow process. Official statistics indicated that in 1987, 7.35 million employees were working under the CLS in state sectors, accounting for 5.6 per cent of total employment. By 1989 there were 11.9 million, accounting for 11.8 per cent (*China Statistical Yearbook*, 1992, p. 117). Thus the majority of employees in state enterprises were still enjoying the 'iron rice bowl'.

6.5 DISCUSSION AND SUMMARY

This chapter has compared the processes of decision making and organizational change in the enterprises in 1984–86 and 1987–88. These processes were lengthy and complex, involving many actors and activities. The processes in both periods shared some similarities. These included 'top-down' procedures, politicization, and design and assessment activities.

Overall, managers in 1987 and 1988 had gained autonomy in organizational design, and decision-making powers had shifted from the party secretary to the directors, but their autonomy was limited by the bureaux. The rigid matrix structure connecting departments in the enterprises with their counterparts in the bureaux hindered change. Moreover the municipal government was able to intervene directly in the enterprises for the purpose of implementing government policies or schemes. With growing enterprise autonomy, such intervention caused conflict between managers and government agencies, as the cases in 1988 have shown. The bureaux remained as the administrative authority in organizational change.

Regarding the relationship between the directors and the Party secretaries, it was the directors who made the decisions while the party secretaries in many enterprises acted as deputies.[10] Furthermore, in 1988 the RLO weakened the overall structure of Party organizations within the enterprises as the number of full-time Party cadres was reduced. But because membership of the executive committee and the Party committee often overlapped, the Party's influence could still be exerted in management.

The role of the Workers' Congress in the decision-making processes needs further study. Although the Congress appears to have been involved in organizational change and in theory gave the final approval, it remains questionable whether or not it had become a rubber-stamp. Industrial relations became the central focus of managers, who tried to maintain good relations with workers and avoid confrontation. This attitude, possibly stemming from the traditional Chinese appreciation of harmonious relations, together with the lack of a social security system, impeded the progress of the RLO.

7 Investment Decision-Making: Product and Production Innovation

7.1 INVESTMENT AS A STRATEGIC DECISION

Investment in production facilities or technological processes is one of the most important decisions for a firm's long-term development. Investment decision making is usually complex and lengthy (Bower, 1970; Butler *et al.*, 1993; Hickson *et al.*, 1986; Yuan Lu and Heard, 1995; Marsh *et al.*, 1988). First, an investment project comes under a firm's business strategy and long-term plan. At the same time the project has its own independent process, comprising a set of activities such as initiation, proposal, design, assessment and approval. However investment decision-making studies note that the initiation stages are crucial, in which ideas are generated, intentions are developed and opportunities are recognized (Marsh *et al.*, 1988; King, 1975). At that stage managers have to incorporate their preferred projects into business strategies or long-term plans and then develop project details.

Second, an investment requires a massive injection of resources, including finance, labour, technology, information and materials. It relies on the commitment and support of those who control resource allocation and have the right to approve the investment. As a result the involvement of internal and external actors with diverse interests and demands becomes unavoidable (Bower, 1970; Yuan Lu and Heard, 1995; Marsh *et al.*, 1988).

Third, the power relations between those at the top and managers are asymmetric. Those at the top have the authority to determine whether or not to proceed with the project, but managers always try to influence them by means of negotiation and bargaining (Bower, 1970; Marsh *et al.*, 1988). It is a political process in which informal behaviour takes place beneath formal procedures and rules. Managers can actually control the flow of information and present a glowing picture of a project to persuade those at the top to accept their ideas (Bower, 1970; Marsh *et al.*, 1988; Pettigrew, 1973).

Investment can be arranged to construct new buildings for the purpose of production expansion, or to improve current production and technology.[1] It can also be concerned with the development of a new product. In China, investment projects, particularly those involving construction, were subject to state approval. Usually three categories of authorities were involved in investment decision-making processes. The first included the industrial bureaux responsible for technological innovation and product development in enterprises. They were also responsible for monitoring investment performance. The second comprised the functional authorities that assessed the feasibility of projects and their impacts on society, such as employment, foreign exchange requirements, compatibility with local construction plans and their effect on the environment. These authorities checked the progress of the projects and some controlled access to resources, such as energy, foreign currency, land and labour. The third consisted of the central planning agencies – government ministries, central planning and economic commissions – which coordinated with other authorities and issued the final authorization. With their approval, the project was recognized as having been incorporated into the state plan.

In addition banks were involved as the source of loans for investment. Credit was advanced by two specialized state-owned banks, the China Investment Bank and the China Industrial and Commercial Bank. The granting of a bank loan to a project depended not only on the bank's own evaluation, but also on final authorization of the project's by the central or local authority.

Before 1985 investment capital came from three sources: state grants, depreciation capital and an enterprise's own funds. Prior to 1985 enterprises handed over all their depreciation capital and profits to the state. Their investment projects were determined by planning authorities, which assigned state grants to the enterprises. This system gradually changed during the decentralization programme. From 1982 the government started to replace grants with bank loans, charging interest.[2] At the same time the government permitted enterprises to retain depreciation capital to fund production development and technology innovation.[3] The depreciation rate increased from an average of 4.1 per cent in 1983 to 4.9 per cent in 1986 (Ministry of Finance, 1988, p. 500). The enterprise's own funds consisted of those from retained profits and credit or loans from financial institutions such as investment corporations. As noted by the China People's Bank, the key investment bank:

After taxation the enterprises have to take 10 to 30 per cent from the production development fund as supplementary capital for current capital. Current capital for new or expanding enterprises is funded by the institution which approves the investment project. Local authorities, government departments and enterprises which arrange their own finance for new construction or expansion of enterprise production capability must provide 30 per cent of the current capital (for commercial firms it is 10 per cent). [After the financing is in place] then, the bank will approve credit (China People's Bank, 1988, p. 507).

The reform of the investment system aimed to create diverse sources of capital and reduce enterprises' dependency on state grants. It also aimed to force enterprises to be responsible for project performance.

In 1984 the central government started to hand over investment-approval power to local government. The SPC lifted its threshold of investment capital from 10 million yuan to 30 million yuan. As a result, local governments had the freedom to decide their investment projects if they were below the SPC's limit, provided they had sufficient sources of finance and the nature of the investment conformed with state policy.[4] The SPC also reformed the project audit system and decreed that large investment projects must be evaluated by its consulting unit.

Decentralization of investment approval to local governments appeared to boost investment activity.[5] Compared with 1983, investment capital in 1984 increased by 21.8 per cent.[6] In 1988, total investment on a national scale increased by 18.5 per cent over that in 1987 (Zhong Chengxun, 1993, p. 97). This rapid increase was pushed by 'investment hunger', the term used by Kornai (1980) to describe the behaviour of firms in a socialist economy. The *Economic Daily* (14 November 1988) reported that local authorities split large projects into a number of smaller ones, each of which was below the SPC's threshold, thus bringing them under the auspices of local government. In this way local governments could avoid the assessment and approval procedures imposed by central government. As Zhang Shaojie and his colleagues (1987) have noted, investment decision making in China was complicated by government intervention. The enterprises and local and central government pursued their own interests, which eventually led to inefficiency and poor results.[7] The World Bank argued that decentralization itself would not ensure efficiency, but that the establishment of fair competition and pricing was more important in guaranteeing the performance of investment projects (World Bank, 1988).

The loss of control over investments contributed to the growth of inflation (Tian Yuan *et al.*, 1989; *Beijing Review*, no. 8, 1989). To control inflation, in 1985 and 1988 the government took measures to recentralize investment approval. These administrative methods included:

• An official programme to re-examine construction projects and cancel non-production investments.
• Freezing new investment projects.
• Reducing bank loans for projects regarded as unimportant to the economy.
• Recentralizing project approval in the SPC.

The effect of these policies and administrative controls was ambiguous. According to newspaper reports, some projects were accelerated in order to complete them before they were frozen by the state (*Economic Daily*, 14 November 1988). Ignoring the State Council's policies, some organizations continued to invest in projects that did not contribute to economic development. Faced with such defiance, the State Council dispatched a number of teams to provinces and municipalities to supervise the implementation of their policies (*Economic Daily*, 20 December 1988).

7.2 TWELVE INVESTMENT DECISIONS IN TWO PHASES

Between 1980 and 1989 the six enterprises studied here experienced two distinct phases of investment decision autonomy. The first phase was from 1980 to 1985. During this period investments were determined by the bureaux and ministries, and state grants were the main source of finance. The second phase was from 1986 to 1989, when the enterprises started to use their own funds and the municipal government became involved in the decision making. Table 7.1 lists the major investment projects promoted by the enterprises from 1980 to 1989.

From 1980 to 1985 the enterprises appeared to have more investment projects than in the later period. Most these involved the introduction of foreign technology or the construction of new workshops. After 1985 some enterprises, including Heavy Electrical, Audio and Electric Switchgear, gradually reduced the scale of their investment. This was partly because they were concentrating on product development and the management of investment projects already introduced; and partly because of the government policy of replacing grants with

Table 7.1 Main investment projects in production facilities and/or new product development schemes in the six enterprises, 1980–89

Enterprise	Key investment projects in production facilities and new product development	Duration
Automotive	1. Introduction of a new model from a Japanese company*	1984–1985
	2. Formation of a joint venture with a Hong Kong company*	1984–88
Audio-Visual	1. Importing an assembly line from a Japanese company	1980–81
	2. Importing an assembly line from a German company	1981–83
	3. Investing in a production workshop*	1983–85
	4. Expansion of production capacity for exports*	1984–86
	5. Importing a process production line from a Japanese company	1988–89
Heavy Electrical	1. Technology transfer from an American company	1983–85
	2. Introduction of a processing line from a German company*	1984–86
	3. Importing a production line and a new product design from a German company	1984–87
	4. Development of a new energy-saving product*	1988
Pharmaceutical	1. Investing in a production workshop to expand production	1981–83
	2. Importing bottling technology*	1985–86
	3. Investing in a production workshop and expansion of production scales*	1987–89
Audio	1. Technology transfer from a Japanese company	1981
	2. Importing a product design from a Hong Kong company*	1983–84
	3. Development of a component for video products*	1985–88
Electric Switchgear	1. Participation of a new product development programme organized by the ministry	1982
	2. Technology transfer of a product design from a German company*	1983–84
	3. A new product development project*	1988

* Projects discussed in this study.

Sources: Data for Heavy Electrical: interviews and documents, October–December 1988 and January–July 1989, MBA project reports 1985, 1986 and 1987 held in CEMI, Beijing. Data for other enterprises: interviews and documents at the enterprises, October–December 1988 and January–July 1989, MBA project reports 1985, 1986, 1987, 1988 and 1989 held in CEMI, Beijing.

bank loans, making it difficult for the enterprises to finance further investments.

Twelve decisions were selected in order to study the changes taking place during the decentralization programme. Table 7.2 presents their contents and investment capital. The six decisions in phase one were initiated and/or completed by 1985; the six in phase two were completed after 1985, five of them in 1988 or 1989. In each phase, three investment decisions concerned production and three concerned new product development.

Duration and Time Framework

The investment decision-making processes varied in duration according to the nature of the project. Large investment projects, such as the construction of new buildings, could be a lengthy process, while new product development might take just a few months. The duration of and the main activities involved in the 12 decisions are shown in Table 7.3.

On average the investment decisions in phase two took longer than those taken in phase one: more than 26 months rather than 20.8. The longest decision-making process was that of Automotive, taking almost four years, from 1984 to 1988. The decision was about forming a joint venture with a Hong Kong company, involving technology transfer, new product design and investment in a new manufacturing site. This will be examined in detail shortly. The duration of decisions on production expansion at Audio-Visual, Heavy Electrical, Audio and Pharmaceutical varied from one to three years. Decisions on product development projects at Heavy Electrical and Electric Switchgear in the second phase were made quite quickly, taking five and seven months respectively. A product development decision at Audio took more than three years, from 1985 to 1988. The decision was about building a new manufacturing line, but it was delayed by the bureau and Audio finally amended the project to developing a component product.

The lengthy process of large investments involved complex activities and two stages. The first stage was the proposal. The enterprise drafted an investment proposal and submitted it to the appropriate authorities – the planning commissions, the municipal government or ministries – for approval. This procedure was time-consuming and problematic. Case studies suggest that many factors could delay approval. For instance, after the SPC introduced a pre-project audit system, carried out by its consulting unit, the assessment procedure could take years. One year of Automotive's investment project, which took

Table 7.2 Investment decisions in phase 1 (pre-1985) and in phase 2 (post-1985)

Enterprise	Investment decisions in phase 1 (pre-1985)	Amount (yuan)	Investment decisions in phase 2 (post-1985)	Amount (yuan)
Automotive	Development of a new model	10 million	Formation of a joint venture and investing in production facilities for inward technology transfer	250 million
Audio-Visual	Construction of a new production line	21 million	Investing in expansion of production capability and establishment of an electronics production site	13 million
Heavy Electrical	Investing in a processing workshop with technology transferred from a German company	1.6 million	New production development	20 000
Pharmaceutical	Investing in a production workshop to expand production scale	3.7 million	Investing in construction of a new production workshop and facilities to increase the scale of production	70 million
Audio	Introduction of a product design and investing in a die-making workshop	2.5 million	Development of a component for video products	35 000
Electric Switchgear	Introduction of product design and production technology from a German company	1.4 million	Modifying an existing product to meet market demand	15 000

Sources: Data for Heavy Electrical: interviews and documents, October–December 1988 and January–July 1989, MBA project reports 1985, 1986 and 1987 at CEMI, Beijing. Data for other enterprises: interviews and documents held in the enterprises, October–December 1988 and January–July 1989, MBA project reports 1985, 1986, 1987, 1988 and 1989 held in CEMI, Beijing.

Table 7.3 Duration and time framework of the 12 investment decisions in phase 1 (pre-1985) and phase 2 (post-1985)

Enterprise	Investment decisions in phase 1 (pre-1985) Duration	Main activities	Investment decisions in phase 2 (post-1985) Duration	Main activities
Automotive	18 months	The project was included in the ministry's long-term plan. The firm and the ministerial research institute worked for one year to finish the design. It took another four months to change the design according to the wishes of the ministry. Final approval was given two months later.	51 months	It took about 10 months for the idea to be included in the state plan. Approval took almost three years. During this time the firm moved its branch factory to a new site and changed its joint-venture partner.
Audio-Visual	18 months	The firm took 14 months to design the production line in the collaboration with the ministry. It took another four months to obtain final approval.	30 months	It took about 10 months to obtain the approval of the SPC. The design and feasibility studies took over one year to finish. The bank also delayed its assessment for about three months.
Heavy Electrical	22 months	It took one year to obtain the approval of the MPC and the MEC delayed about six months. Negotiations with the bank took about four months.	5 months	It took just one month for the product design and another four months to obtain the Municipal Science and Technology Commission's approval.

Pharmaceutical	24 months	It took more than one year to obtain the approval of the bureau and the SPC, and another one year for the feasibility study to be accepted.	25 months	It took about nine months for the project to be included in the municipal development plan. The MPC was quick to give approval, but it took more than a year to obtain the approval of the various functional bureaux.
Audio	31 months	The project design was delayed by the ministerial research institute. Thus it took almost two years for the proposal to be approved. The rest of the time was spent on the feasibility study.	41 months	The proposal was first dismissed by the bureau. Then, it was resubmitted two years later. It took almost nine months for the director to come to a decision on the issue.
Electric Switchgear	12 months	The first four months were spent on negotiations with the ministry. The other eight months were spent on proposal preparation and the feasibility study.	7 months	It took about three months for the market investigation. The final decision was taken four months later.
Average	20.8 months		26.5 months	

Sources: Data for Heavy Electrical: interviews and documents, October–December 1988 and January–July 1989, MBA project reports 1985, 1986 and 1987 at CEMI, Beijing. Data for other enterprises: interviews and documents held in the enterprises, October–December 1988 and January–July 1989, MBA project reports 1985, 1986, 1987, 1988 and 1989 held in CEMI, Beijing.

from 1984 to 1988 to decide upon, was spent on completing this routine assessment. Such a delay could also occur if the interests of the enterprises and authorities conflicted. This was particularly true in the case of Audio.

The second stage was approval of the feasibility study. The enterprises had to present technical details concerning construction design, market surveys and investment budgeting. It usually took less time to have the feasibility study approved. This was the final authorization, after which the project could be included in the state's annual construction plan.

The involvement of actors in these investment decisions was determined by two factors – the nature and the amount of the investment.

Authorizing authority	Investment threshold (yuan)
The State Council	> 200 million
The SPC	30–200 million
Ministry/municipal government	1–30 million
Industrial bureaux	< 1 million

Note: These thresholds were adjusted according to state policy and the nature of the project. For instance Pharmaceutical's investment, proposed in 1987–89, was approved by the MPC rather than the SPC, although the application was for 70 million yuan, which was above the municipal government authorization level. The reason was that the project was not strategic, and the investment capital was raised by local authorities without SPC grants.

The following were the thresholds of investment approval in 1988:

Enterprise	Authorizing authority	
	Phase 1 (pre-1985)	Phase 2 (post-1985)
Automotive	Industrial ministry	State council
Audio-Visual	Industrial ministry	SPC
Heavy Electrical	SEC and industrial ministry	Municipal Science and Technology Commission
Pharmaceutical	MPC	MPC
Audio	MPC	Director
Electric Switchgear	Industrial ministry	Director

These thresholds determined the level at which final authorization was given. The 12 decisions were thus approved at the following levels: The enterprises' autonomy in investment decision making varied. All the phase 1 decisions were approved by the authorities, in phase 2 directors approved two decisions. Before 1985 any change in production facilities or products required permission from a bureau or ministry. The most centralized case was Automotive's phase 2 investment proposal, in which the final authority was the State Council because of the large amount of investment capital involved. Thus enterprise autonomy was limited, and authorities still exerted control over investment.

Before final approval was given many other government agencies functioned as assessors in investment decisions. Table 7.4 lists the actors involved in the 12 decisions. Table 7.4 reveals the complexity of investment decision making caused by the involvement of various authorities, each of which held power of approval. Automotive's investment decision (1984–88) involved some outside firms, which the municipal government and ministry had instructed to join the project as suppliers and coordinators. Decisions concerning new product development might involve the ministry's research institutes – as happened in the cases of Automotive and Heavy Electrical – to set product standards and support technological innovation.

Of the internal actors, technicians and technical managers were crucial as they were the initiators of product development and investment in production facilities. They carried out project design and feasibility studies. At the project design and selection stage management normally provided details of the technological design; wrote reports; organized feasibility study missions, market assessment trips and conferences; and made arrangements for new technology, the hiring of labour and the securing of supplies. Interestingly, only in large firms were financial managers consulted in project design. In most cases it was the technical managers who made the financial analyses of the investment. Ironically, no sales department personnel participated in the decision making, market surveys being conducted by technical managers.

7.3 DEPENDENCE ON THE PLANNING AUTHORITIES

Any large investment in production facilities had to be included in a ministry or industrial bureau's five-year plan, which was in turn incorporated into state plans. Plans or assignments from the planning authorities encouraged enterprises to embark on such investments, as the

Table 7.4 Actors involved and their functions in the 12 investment decisions

Enterprise	Number of decisions involved (N=6 for each group)		Main functions
	In phase 1 (pre-1985)	In phase 2 (post-1985)	
External:			
State Council	–	1	To approve Automotive's project, 1984–88.
SPC	1	2	To approve strategic projects, as in Automotive and Audio-Visual's proposals.
SEC	1	1	To approve technological innovation, as in Heavy Electrical's proposal in phase 1 and Automotive's investment in phase 2.
The ministries	2	4	To approve projects under long-term plans and technology transfer, as in Automotive's and Audio-Visual's projects, and Heavy Electrical and Electric Switchgear's proposals in phase 1.
Municipal government	–	1	Only in that of Pharmaceutical, as it was important for the municipal government's strategic project.
MPC	3	3	To approve municipal investment, as in Pharmaceutical. It also approved large investment projects such as Audio-Visual's and Automotive's.
MEC	3	3	To approve technological innovation, as in Pharmaceutical's and Heavy Electrical's projects in phase 1. It also approved large investment projects involving technology transfer, as in Audio-Visual's projects and Automotive's proposal, 1984–88.
Industrial bureaux	6	6	To approve most investment projects and technology innovation projects.
Functional bureaux	1	4	To assess the impact of an investment projects on the community, infrastructure and environment. Not involved in the two product development projects at Heavy Electrical and Electric Switchgear in phase 2.

Banks	2	4	To assess applications for bank loans for investment. Not involved in projects with enterprises' own funds, such as Heavy Electrical's and Electric Switchgear's product developments in phase 2.
Investment corporations	–	1	Only in Automotive as an investment partner.
Others	–	2	Ministerial research institutes were for design and assessment. The Municipal Science and Technology Commission approved Heavy Electrical's project in 1988. The SPC's consulting unit was involved in the assessment of Automotive and Audio-Visual. A number of firms were involved in Automotive's projects as coordinators and suppliers.

Internal:

Director	6	6	To give first approval of the investment proposal and organize the assessment procedure.
Deputy directors	6	6	To organize project design and selection within the firm.
Technology department	6	6	To design new products and/or product technology transfer procedures.
Planning department	5	4	To draw up the enterprise investment plan and coordinate with the bureau/ministry.
Production department	3	3	To assess production capability and provide relevant information.
Finance department	2	2	To help technicians to draft the investment budget proposal.
Supply department	–	1	Only in Automotive's proposal, 1984–88: to provide data regarding supplies.
Personnel department	–	1	Only in Automotive's proposal, 1984–88: to provide data regarding labour supply.
Construction department	2	3	To draw up a construction plan for inclusion in the feasibility study report.

Sources: Data for Heavy Electrical: interviews and documents, October–December 1988 and January–July 1989, MBA project reports 1985, 1986 and 1987 at CEMI, Beijing. Data for other enterprises: interviews and documents held in the enterprises, October–December 1988 and January–July 1989, MBA project reports 1985, 1986, 1987, 1988 and 1989 held in CEMI, Beijing.

cases of Automotive and Audio-Visual revealed. Even where an investment was in product innovation, the planning authorities could still play the initiating role, as was found at Heavy Electrical. The Municipal Science and Technology Commission wanted to promote the development of a new energy-saving product, and asked Heavy Electrical to develop it. The Commission then supplied the necessary finance and instructed local enterprises to accept the product.

Enterprises relied upon resources controlled by the planning authorities. Before 1985 all investment projects were dependent upon state grants, and only a small proportion of finance came from other sources. This changed after 1985, when bank loans became the major source of investment finance. Table 7.5 summarizes sources of funding before and after 1985.

After 1985, an enterprise's financial dependency on the planning authorities was only partially reduced. An enterprise's own funds from depreciation and retained profits were usually not sufficient to support investment. At the same time, bank loans were still dependent on quotas or permission from the planning commissions. It was virtually impossible to obtain a bank loan if a project was not included in the state investment plan.

Moreover the financial reliance of enterprises on the planning authorities was also evident in the market prospects, as products linked to an investment would be placed on the ministry's approved list. Enterprises that were chosen to implement ministry or bureau projects had secure distribution channels. For instance, the Municipal Science and Technology Commission required local customers to purchase Heavy Electrical's new product. This was critical for the performance of the investment. In contrast, Audio proposed to invest in video products, but the proposal did not suit the bureau's plan. The enterprise carried on with the project, but this proved difficult because Audio lacked both financial resources and the support of the authorities with regard to obtaining a new business license to sell and trade the video products. Because of these problems, the project was finally abandoned and a component was produced instead.

Finally, the authorities and official consulting units were additional factors in determining whether or not a project should be implemented. Enterprise managers were obliged to alter the content of their proposal or design whenever an authority requested it, regardless of how impractical this was. As the chief engineer of Pharmaceutical said: 'We changed the details of our report each time we met with a bureau. When the electricity bureau questioned our estimates for electricity

Table 7.5 Sources of investment funding

Enterprise	Investment in phase 1 (pre-1985)		Investment in phase 2 (post-1985)	
	Total investment (yuan)	Source	Total investment (yuan)	Source
Automotive	10 million	25% bank loans 25% ministry grants 50% internal funds	250 million	60% bank loans 25% joint-venture partners 25% internal
Audio-Visual	21 million	60% bank loans 40% ministry grants and internal	13 million	90% bank loans 1% ministry grants 9% internal
Heavy Electrical	1.6 million	75% bank loans 7% ministry grants 18% internal	20 thousand	Grants from the Municipal Science and Technology Commission
Pharmaceutical	3.7 million	90% bank loans 10% internal	70 million	90% bank loans 10% internal
Audio	2.5 million	61% bank loans 39% internal	35 thousand	Internal
Electric Switchgear	1.4 million	60% ministry grants 40% bank loans	15 thousand	Internal

Sources: Data for Heavy Electrical: interviews and documents, October–December 1988 and January–July 1989, MBA project reports 1985, 1986 and 1987 held in CEMI, Beijing. Data for other enterprises: interviews and documents held in the enterprises, October–December 1988 and January–July 1989, MBA project reports 1985, 1986, 1987, 1988 and 1989 held in CEMI, Beijing.

demand, we decreased the figure.' The tacit understanding was that a failure to accept the electricity bureau's view would mean that the additional power supply needed for the new investment would not be forthcoming.

This process could impose a significant burden on an enterprise, as the controls exercised by external authorities at all stages of the investment decision process caused considerably delays. Nevertheless the first response of an enterprise was to seize an opportunity to bid for a project formulated by a ministry. As a manager at Audio-Visual said, it was a question of 'dive in first and worry about the details later'. Internal discussions of projects normally took a matter of weeks, but securing external approval could take years.

The bureaux set the conditions for investment decisions while the enterprises mainly carried out routine procedures. Although the relationship between the higher authorities and the enterprises appears to have been very asymmetrical, in practice managers were able to secure some initiative by dint of their superior technological knowledge.

Enterprises within the same industrial sector competed for project assignments. Here, personal relations (*guanxi*) and an enterprise's link to the ministries and/or bureaux emerged as powerful tools. For instance, on economic grounds Audio-Visual was not the optimum location for expanding the production of a particular product type, but it was selected nonetheless. This was partly because its director had formerly worked in the industrial bureau for many years and consequently had established close personal ties with key persons in the bureau and the ministry. Another factor was that the ministry favoured the investment being conducted close to it in Beijing, so that its officials could monitor the project easily.

Managers could ignore market information and rely on information supplied by the authorities, but they preferred to listen to the opinions of their sales staff, although it was apparent that these opinions were not always systematically collected and analysed. There was considerable scepticism about the value of market research in a situation where sudden changes in government policy could negate the research. Reliance on information from the authorities was associated with the process of securing final approval for investment expenditure. By accepting investment projects initiated by the authorities, managers were consciously avoiding the conflict that would arise from a difference between their own information sources and the authority's investment intentions.

A typical example was identified in Pharmaceutical. The enterprise assigned a team of MBA students to conduct a market survey. The results suggested that the enterprise should maintain an annual production level of around 300 million units. This forecast was based on total market size and the competitive positions of the main producers, and was close to what managers thought because it was consistent with the reports of sales staff and the growth rates of sales in the past few years. When municipal government senior officials visited the enterprise they recommended expanding production capacity to 500 million units a year. Although many managers agreed with the market survey, the enterprise adopted the higher figure for its investment budget. As one manager said, the size of the budget was determined by the municipal government, which preferred large-scale investment. If the enterprise had followed the MBA team's suggestion, the project would have been cancelled because the officials would have considered it was not worth investing in. When the project was completed in 1990 competition was strong, with more than 400 competitors, and Pharmaceutical had to reduce production. Thus the MBA team's survey was a more accurate forecast of the market than that of the authorities.

7.4 LARGE INVESTMENT PROJECTS: A CASE STUDY OF AUTOMOTIVE

Of the 12 investment decision proposals, that of Automotive, which took from 1984 to 1988, was the longest and most centralized. As the project exceeded the budget limit of the SPC, final approval had to come from the State Council. A complex process, the decision consisted of many subdecisions, and its content was altered several times in order to fit the requirements of different authorities. Details of this process are outlined below.

In early 1984 the Ministry of Machine Building and the municipal government both planned to establish a large-scale production site in Beijing. For the municipal government, the development of the automotive industry was a long-term strategy. During early 1984 the ministry was eager to develop a new product model licensed by a Japanese company. It wanted to renew product design and production technology and Automotive was part of that programme. A team of technicians from Automotive collaborated with the ministry's research institute on this new venture. In 1985 the enterprise started trial production of the new model. The aim was for Automotive to take the lead and integrate other local firms into the programme.

The project was included in the ministry's long-term plan. In November 1984 three commissions – the SPC, the SEC and the SCRES – and the Ministry of Machine Building jointly organized a national conference to discuss industrial strategy. At the conference Automotive was selected as one of three automotive production sites certified by the ministry. The SPC then instructed the firm to continue the technology transfer from the Japanese company and increase its production to meet market demand. The investment was formally approved and the investment plan was included in the State Council's Seventh Five-Year Plan (1986–90). The enterprise then began to outline its investment proposal. From 1984 to 1988 several important events influenced the project. Table 7.6 charts the progress of the decision.

The initial idea was to modify Automotive's product, derived from licensed Japanese technology, and increase its production capability by renewing its facilities. In order to achieve this Automotive required large resource inputs. The first was a site at which to relocate its manufacturing facilities. The municipal government helped in this by enabling Automotive to take over a local factory.

However the most serious problem was financing the investment. It was estimated that Automotive would require more than one billion yuan to renew its dated technology and production facilities. Neither the municipal government nor the ministry had sufficient resources. Moreover, as 1984 was a critical year in the decentralization programme the state discouraged state grants as investment capital. The ministry therefore asked the enterprise to seek funds from two sources. The first was from the newly established investment corporations. The second was to form a joint venture with foreign investors, and the ministry introduced an US company as a potential partner.

In October 1984 the director approached the chief executive of a national investment corporation, a former university colleague. Their relationship, another example of *guanxi*, was an important factor in promoting their collaboration, as the corporation quickly agreed to supply investment capital. The municipal government and the ministry attracted other partners for the project, including two other ministries and a number of firms. They formed an alliance to provide capital and raw materials. The total investment capital was to be 1.1 billion yuan. During 1985 a team of technicians and planning managers, plus a number of staff from various institutions, worked together to complete the proposal.

The proposal was altered several times. It was first submitted to the industrial bureau, the MPC, the MEC and the ministry. In early 1985 the municipal government and the ministry organized two working

Table 7.6 Chronicle of investment decision making in Automotive, 1984–88

Date	Main events
Spring 1984	The ministry assigned a new product model (licensed by a Japanese company) to Automotive.
October 1984	Collaborative programme with a national investment corporation.
November 1984	Three state commissions and the ministry drew up the long-term development strategy of the automotive industry. Automotive was selected as a key manufacturer. The ministry also introduced a potential partner to negotiate the formation of a joint venture.
Autumn 1984	Acquisition of a local factory as a new manufacturing site with the help of the municipal government.
March–August 1985	Preparation of the investment proposal report. The ministry organized two seminars to assess the content.
October 1985	Submission of the proposal to the SPC.
November 1985	SPC's consulting unit assessed the proposal. The SPC instructed the proposal be altered.
May 1985–October 1986	The firm started moving its manufacturing workshops to the new site.
March 1986	New investment proposal prepared and submitted to the ministry.
1986–87	Negotiations between the firm, the investment corporation and the Hong Kong partner.
December 1987	The SPC approved the proposal, but ordered a reduction in the amount of investment.
March 1988	Feasibility study report and construction design approved.
March 1988	Joint venture contract approved.

Sources: Interviews and documents held in Automotive, October–December 1988 and January–July 1989; MBA project reports 1985, 1986, 1987, 1988 and 1989 held in CEMI, Beijing.

seminars to assess the proposal. At the same time negotiations with a US company were in progress. In October 1985 the proposal was submitted to the SPC, and the SPC's project audit agency, an official consulting unit, took over the evaluation of the proposal. In November 1986, one year after the proposal had been submitted, the SPC reached its decision. It rejected the joint-venture proposal, but suggested the enterprise modify its manufacturing facilities. The SPC had become cautious because the automotive market was in recession during 1985. The decline in sales was caused by the state's austerity drive, which had reduced the capital supply. The SPC had other reasons for rejecting the proposal – there had been four proposals for similar products, and the SPC believed that the sum involved was too large.

However, while the SPC was evaluating the project Automotive had already moved one branch factory to the new site. With the support of the municipal government it persisted with its joint-venture plans because this would give it full autonomy in foreign trade over imported key materials and the exportation of finished products. The investment corporation agreed to use its Hong Kong company as the foreign partner. The amount of the investment was reduced to 600 million yuan, and Automotive submitted its revised proposal to the SPC in March 1986 for assessment.

During 1987 and early 1988 the SPC and the ministries had a number of discussions on the project and finally approved it in December 1987, although the investment capital was reduced to 250 million yuan. The feasibility study report was approved in March 1988. One month later the State Commission for Foreign Economy and Trade approved the joint-venture contract. Construction for the project then started.

During the four-year period the project involved 25 organizations, including the State Council, four state commissions, three ministries, three municipal government agencies, the industrial bureau and five functional bureaux, two ministries research institutes and six other firms as suppliers and coordinators, in addition to the investment corporation, the Hong Kong company and two banks. Such a large investment project was thus very complex and lengthy.

Another example was Audio-Visual's proposal, authorized in 1986. This project too had been initiated by the ministry, and again the amount of investment capital was reduced, from 19 million yuan to 13 million. The approval involved three state commissions, three ministries, two municipal commissions and two bureaux. The project involved purchasing a piece of land upon which to build a new workshop, which would have to have the approval of the bureau of land property and the city construction programme. In order to avoid further bureaucratic procedures, the ministries and the bureaux finally abandoned the land-purchasing plan, but decided to reform an old production workshop at the existing Audio-Visual site.

Compared with the situation before 1985, investment projects in the second phase were more constrained by the functional authorities. According to the head of the enterprise reform department at the Municipal Commission for Restructuring the Economic System, during phase 1 the key authorities in investment project approval were the planning and economic commissions, the industrial ministries and local industrial bureaux. But in 1986 this list had extended to include project audit agencies (official consulting units), functional bureaux, banks and other institutions relevant to the project. For instance an investment involving construction had to be assessed by the Municipal Construction Planning Bureau, and production expansion investment needed the permission of the Electricity Bureau, which assigned electricity quotas to industrial firms. Other bureaux involved were those dealing with environmental protection, transport, water supply, and labour and personnel. The planning commissions gave final approval only after all authorities had agreed.

Therefore during phase 2 the functional bureaux emerged as the power centres, weakening the status of the industrial ministries and bureaux, and lengthening the decision-making process. Even when a project was initiated by the municipal government, delays or interruptions could take place, as shown in the case of Pharmaceutical. The enterprise won an award from the municipal government for its record exports. Therefore in 1987, when the MPC and the MEC drew up a local industrial development strategy, Pharmaceutical was selected to promote foreign trade. In October 1987 a team of senior officials from the municipal government visited the enterprise and, impressed by its achievements, immediately decided to support an upgrade in production. This project was fully financed by the MPC. Although the central government agencies were not involved, the process was still complex as the MPC did not have the resources to finance the project. It took more than two years to secure these. The proposal ended up obtaining 46 seals of approval from various authorities before the MPC gave its final consent.

7.5. NEW PRODUCT DEVELOPMENT: AN INCREASE IN
ENTERPRISE AUTONOMY

No investment decisions occurring before 1985 were approved by an
enterprise director. After 1985 there were two cases – at Audio and
Electric Switchgear – where the approval of the planning authorities
was not required. Both dealt with product development, and were small
enough to be funded by the enterprises themselves. This indicates that
enterprises could approve their own projects as long as the problem of
financing was solved.

Audio's project was initiated mid-1985 by the associated bureau,
which wanted to develop video products. Several local firms, including Audio, bid for the project. Audio was in a weak position because
it produced audio rather than video products. Audio pointed out that it
had obtained audio technology from a Japanese company, and that it
would not be difficult to alter this for video production. However the
project was assigned to another local firm. Then the bureau offered
Audio the chance of being a supplier to the project. Although the director persisted in trying to develop video products, it was impossible
because the bureau and the ministry strictly controlled video production.

The project proposed by the bureau was slowed down by lack of
capital and key technology. During 1986 and 1987 Audio supplied
only sample components and then had no further orders from the main
firm. In late 1987 the director of Audio learnt from a conference organized by the ministry that the domestic video market had to rely on
imports because local manufacturers were unable to compete with foreign
products in quantity and quality. Audio then resubmitted its proposal
for video products. By now, with decentralization progressing, the bureau
was no longer able to control Audio. The enterprise was able to proceed with its plan, but it proved difficult. For instance Audio's business license did not permit it to produce and sell video products. Because
the bureau had not fully approved Audio's product change, the Municipal Industry and Commerce Bureau withheld the new business license. More serious was the enterprise's inability to obtain sufficient
financing. No bank was willing to give credit to a project without the
approval of the authorities. In September 1988 the project was amended
to producing a component and supplying it to other video manufacturers.
In 1993 the enterprise was still unable to manufacture video products,
so the proposal was dropped.

Managers at Audio complained that they could have been very successful if the bureau had approved their plan in 1985. However, as this case demonstrates, enterprise autonomy could be constrained by resources and access to the market. Lack of finance was the main problem for most enterprises. Heavy Electrical reported that its new product development fund, drawn from retained profits, was not sufficient to support new product tests. Smaller enterprises were in a worse situation. Electric Switchgear, for instance, was assigned two projects by the ministry in the early 1980s to renew its product design and update production technology. But from 1986 it had to draw a halt because of a lack of money. Its technological innovation was limited to modifying existing products.

7.6. DISCUSSION AND SUMMARY

The investment decisions studied in this chapter remained heavily dependent upon the planning authorities even after the issuing of regulations giving enterprises the right to allocate investment funds. Ministries and bureaux continued to be major initiators of proposals, encouraging enterprises to bid first and work out a feasibility study later.

This continued dependency of the enterprises upon the planning authorities and governmental agencies for funding, especially in the case of large investments, and the intervention of the authorities in the initiation and approval of projects meant that the enterprises were not yet sufficiently autonomous to be technologically innovative. Although in the second phase enterprise managers had some autonomy in determining product development, investment remained under external control. When the enterprises themselves were able to fund small projects, their dependency was reduced and their autonomy increased. But owing to the scarcity of internal funds, it was difficult for the enterprises to undertake strategic investment.[8]

The involvement of the authorities implies that the state controlled investment projects by setting an industrial development policy that was used as a guideline for long-term planning.[9] A number of enterprises were selected to further the state plan, and they enjoyed government support in financing and other areas. The findings in this study are consistent with other investigations. For instance Yuan Lu and Heard (1995) found that large projects had to be adjusted according to policies or guidelines drawn up by the SPC or relevant ministries. Moreover the state also limited the amount of investment. Large projects were required to have the permission of the SPC or even the State Council. Yuan Lu and Heard also found that personal relations were extensively used to facilitate project approval. The state enterprises thus remained locked into the structure of the higher authorities (c.f. Blecher, 1989). The restrictions set by the planning authorities demonstrated certain inefficiencies. Continued dependence on external institutions diverted investment decision making away from economic rationality. First, it enhanced the role of personal influence as a decision criterion. Second, it maintained the enterprise's dependence on the planning authorities for technical and market information, the latter often proving inaccurate and resulting in below optimum investment decisions. Cases where the information provided by an authority was different from that directly available to the enterprise only added to the uncertainty. Third, considerable time was wasted on the decision-making process, especially when there was conflict or poor coordination between the different authorities.

Partial economic decentralization has created a more complex investment environment. The delegation of investment approval to local government forced the enterprises to deal more closely with local authorities. Furthermore the introduction of specialized bureaux, each having some power of intervention over investment projects, led to multiple supervision, as Granick (1990) has noted.

The cases studied in this chapter also suggest a negotiating relationship between the authorities and the enterprises. Although the enterprises depended on the authorities for resources, the authorities depended on the enterprises to realize investment projects profitably in order to provide tax revenues and contributions to community welfare. Enterprise managers could gain some control over resources through their superior technological knowledge. The process was facilitated through bargaining and negotiation, using personal contacts and relations within the bureaucratic framework.

8 Summary, Current Reform of State Enterprises and Conclusions

8.1 SUMMARY OF RESEARCH FINDINGS IN THE PREVIOUS CHAPTERS

In the proceeding chapters, five kinds of decision and their processes have been studied, namely purchasing, pricing, recruitment, organizational change and investment in production or product development. For each kind, two decisions in each of the six enterprises have been compared. Consequently a total of 60 decisions have been examined. These decisions were selected from two periods: pre-1985, when the decentralization programme started, and during 1988–89.

As a result of the decentralization programme the decision-making context in 1988 differed from that in 1985 with regard to relations between the enterprises and the planning authorities, the development of the market and the status of Communist Party organizations within the enterprises. These changes had an impact on the decision-making processes. A comparison of decision-making contexts and processes is made in Table 8.1.

Purchasing decisions are viewed as operational. By 1988–89 planning authorities such as the ministries and bureaux had shifted their area of control from the direct arrangement of procurement to the allocation of planning quotas of strategic materials. As a result the enterprises started to enjoy far greater autonomy when selecting suppliers. The decision-making process could be quick and simple when purchasing from the market, but whenever a planning authority was involved it could become complex.

Decisions regarding product prices proved more complex. In general, because the state reduced its pricing monopoly over industrial products the enterprises had obtained greater autonomy by 1988. But their powers could be limited by two constraints. The first was direct intervention by ministries or bureaux if a product was regarded as strategic, forcing the enterprises to follow state-set prices. The second was the interference of the functional authorities, such as the pricing

Table 8.1 Characteristics of the five kinds of decision and their processes

Purchasing decisions:

	1985	*1988–89*
Decision context	Highly dependent upon state plans, and ministries/bureaux directly delivered supplies. Little market coordination, but stable delivery and prices.	Coexistence of state plans and partial market. The state controlled strategic materials with planning quotas, uncertainty in delivery and prices.
Decision processes	Followed the state plan, smoothly and simply as routine tasks. Ministries or bureaux approved purchases when the supply was subject to the state control. Enterprises had no autonomy.	Mainly followed enterprise choice, but the purchase of strategic materials depended on the ministry's or bureau's planning quotas.
	Market supplies were determined by managers.	Managers had much more autonomy to choose supply sources and suppliers.

Pricing a product:

	1985	*1988–89*
Decision context	The state controlled most prices and there were few market-price determination mechanisms.	Dual price systems with state, float and market prices, depending on whether or not the product was controlled by the state. Functional authorities started to play an important role in auditing and intervening in enterprise pricing policies.
Decision processes	Lengthy and involving the authorities. Enterprises had little autonomy, unless the product was fully open to the market.	Lengthy and involving the authorities. Enterprises had more autonomy when more products were relaxed. The state prices were usually in conflict with the market ones.

Recruitment:

	1985	1988–89
Decision context	Recruitment was part of the state policy encouraging full employment. The state directly allocated recruitment quotas.	The state controlled the wage/salary budget. Bureaux provided information and services.
Decision processes	Followed the state plan and required the bureaux to allocate quotas.	Followed the enterprise plan. Enterprises had most autonomy in deciding the number of employees and the selection procedure.

Organizational change:

	1984 and 1986	1987–88
Decision context	The state adopted the DRS in state enterprises and decision-making powers were transferred from the Party secretaries to the directors. The matrix structure with the bureau limited enterprise power to alter the organizational structure.	The municipal government launched the RLO scheme and forced the enterprises to lay off redundant workers. Managers had the power to design the structure, but their autonomy was limited by bureau intervention. Matrix structure still existed.
Decision processes	Lengthy and involving the bureaux, a top-down process starting with political training. Party secretaries started to lose their powers.	Lengthy and involving the bureaux, a top-down process with political training and pilot programmes. The Party organizations were reduced. The directors dominated decision making.

continued on page 156

Table 8.1 continued

Investment in production and product development:		
	Before 1985	*After 1985*
Decision context	The state controlled funds and projects. Enterprises had no autonomy. Most investment capital was provided by government grants.	Diverse sources of funding from bank loans, government grants and enterprises' own funds. Large projects were controlled by the planning authorities. The enterprises had some autonomy to develop a product with their own funds.
Decision processes	Lengthy and complex, involving many authorities. Investment was initiated and arranged by ministries or bureaux as part of state plans.	Lengthy and more complex because of the involvement of numerous authorities, especially functional ones. Large-scale investment was initiated and arranged according to the state plan, but product development could be undertaken by the enterprises.

bureau, which carried out state policies through administrative control of the economy, for instance reducing inflation by freezing commodity prices. This second constraint had a greater effect on pricing decisions.

Recruitment decisions were the ones in which the enterprises had most autonomy. They appeared to be routine and followed annual recruitment plans. None of the decisions during 1988–89 required the bureaux authorization and managers had the power to select and determine the number of new employees. The role of the bureaux was in most cases confined to the provision of information, communication and coordination.

Organizational change was a complex issue. As Chapter 6 has shown, managers had little power when a change attempted to alter relations with the bureaux and/or modify Party organizations within the enterprises. A comparison of the decisions in the two periods has shown that government schemes such as the DRS from 1984 to 1986 and the RLO in 1988 were significant stimuli forcing the enterprises to change. Thus organizational changes within enterprises were caused by external social–political pressures. Moreover, since the directors were usually Party committee members, and since Party secretaries often doubled as deputy directors, enterprise management was part of the political–economic complex governed by the state and the Party.

Investment decisions were the most centralized. Unless involved in self-funded product development the enterprises had little autonomy when determining strategic investment projects. The enterprises not only had to rely on the resources of the planning authorities, but also on access to the market and the approval of the functional authorities. The decision-making processes post-1985 grew lengthier and more complex because of the involvement of functional authorities, who assessed proposals. Large investments were still controlled by the state or municipal government agencies.

The significance of the findings of the 60 case studies is that the success of the decentralization programme was contingent on the nature of the decisions taken. Decisions that were of an operational nature, such as recruitment and purchasing, were more easily decentralized to lower levels. Decisions of a more strategic nature, such as prices, organizational change and large investments, were more difficult to decentralize. This argument is consistent with other findings that note that decentralization is dynamic and the delegation of decision making is usually contingent on the strategic importance of the decision. Some decisions are delegated, others are not. Decisions considered unimportant are usually delegated, but strategic decisions often remain centralized (Jennergren, 1981). Consequently production decisions are usually the first to be delegated, and sales decisions are often delegated when a firm is growing in size. Financial decisions and strategic investment are controlled by the top (ibid.) Some decisions (for example organizational change and strategic investment) present very complex processes and are usually centralized, even when taken in a market economy (Hickson *et al.*, 1986; Yuan Lu and Heard, 1995).[1]

Decentralization is also limited by 'soft-budgetary constraints' (Kornai, 1980). As a result the enterprises studied were torn between bureaux commands and market demands. This was similar to what happened during the reforms in former Eastern European countries (Kornai, 1980, 1986, 1989; Montias, 1988). It proved that the old institutional framework, which was established for the purpose of state control and a

centrally planned economic administration, was resistant to decentralization. Such resistance could be overcome only through a wider reform
of the institutional framework, which was beyond the scope of the
decentralization programme.[2] Thus, under the planned economy and
partial market reform, decentralization alone was unable to improve
the performance of state enterprises.

8.2 CURRENT REFORM OF STATE ENTERPRISES

From 1987 to 1992 the CRS was the principal scheme in the reform
of state enterprises.[3] However, the effectiveness of the CRS as a measure
to improve state enterprise performance was unreliable. In 1988 more
than 95 per cent of the enterprises adhering to the CRS fulfilled their
profit contracts. In 1989 this had declined to less than 80 per cent, and
in 1990 to less than 70 per cent.[4] This was partly because the reform
was halted after mid-1989 when the pro-democracy movement in Beijing
was crushed. Up to 1992 the focus of state policies was on implementing the CRS,[5] and local governments tested various decentralization
programmes.[6]

The year 1992 was critical for the progress of the reforms in China.
In early 1992 Deng Xiaoping visited southern China and delivered a
series of speeches. He encouraged 'bolder reform' and argued that a
market economy was compatible with state socialism.[7] His speeches
led to renewed praise of the market economy[8] and provoked a rapid
change of policy, the partial market programme being replaced by
comprehensive markets (*Beijing Review*, no. 42, 1992; Fang Sheng,
1992).

Unlike previous policies, the reform programme after 1992 attempted
to restructure the enterprise management system by transforming state
enterprises into independent business units. Thus in July 1992 the State
Council published 'Regulation on the Changes in the Operating Mechanisms of State-Owned Enterprises' (*guanyu zhuanhuan guoying qiye
jingying jizhi de guiding*). The central theme of this policy was to
delegate 14 decision-making powers to enterprises in the following
areas: production planning, pricing, purchasing, foreign trade, investment, use of retained profits, disposal of fixed assets, formation of
alliances with other firms, employment recruitment and selection, personnel management, labour management, allocation of wages and bonuses,
organizational design and change and the right to refuse funds, materials and services allocated by government agencies (*Beijing Review*,

nos 24, 26, 46, 1992). The reform after 1992 was aimed at clarifing the ownership structure and introducing a new enterprise governance based on the market economy.[9] Attention then shifted from the level of decision making to ownership.[10]

How much has been achieved remains questionable. Between 1979 and 1993 the growth rate of state enterprises only averaged 8 per cent a year, less than those of township and private enterprises, which achieved about 35 per cent and 60 per cent respectively (Ma Hong and Sun Shangqing, 1994). In 1991 it was reported that only 30 per cent of the enterprises that had adopted the CRS were able to fulfil their contracts, while the majority failed to meet their contract targets (Wu Zhenkun and Chen Wentong, 1993, p. 131). At the end of 1992, 45 per cent of state enterprises declared a loss (Liu Zishen and Sun Yong, 1993). In November 1994 the reported losses incurred were 27.5 per cent, higher than in 1993 (*People's Daily*, 31 December 1994). The actual situation could be much worse. It was estimated that in 1990 about 70–80 per cent of state enterprises had hidden losses, that is, bad debts and a considerable waste of materials and human resources that were not revealed by official statistics (*China's Reform and Development Report 1992–1993*). A survey conducted by the China Industrial Economic Association during January and February 1994 indicated that many state enterprises suffered from intervention by local governments and/or various governmental agencies, which interfered in decision-making and used enterprise resources for their own benefit.[11] Furthermore state enterprises had to bear heavy social welfare costs.[12] All these weakened the enterprises' competitive positions in the market and their economic performance.

8.3 UPDATE ON THE SIX ENTERPRISES IN 1993

Following the State Council's policy on operating mechanisms in state enterprises in July 1992, the Beijing municipal government accelerated the pace of decentralization. In addition to having the power to decide on routine operations, the enterprises were now in charge of foreign trade and investment.[13] In 1992 and 1993 the municipal government further amended its measures concerning the CRS and enterprise decision-making autonomy by bestowing enterprises with the status given to joint ventures (conferring tax and regulatory advantages).

Enterprise managers, some of whom had taken part in the research in 1985 and 1988, were interviewed during the summer of 1993.[14]

Table 8.2 identifies the size, financial profile and official category of the six enterprises, and whether or not production was geared to a quota or a profit target. As can be seen, by 1993 all the enterprises were open to the market and none had production quotas, a result of the sharp decline in state control. Apart from this, the six enterprises exhibited diverse growth rates and business development strategies.

Three of the enterprises were in the large-size category: Automotive, Audio-Visual and Heavy Electrical, the latter becoming a large firm after acquiring three local factories. They enjoyed strong state support and had expanded noticeably in sales, profitability and employment. Automotive's investment in 1984–88 had enabled the enterprise to become a market leader. Audio-Visual had taken over its local competitor and three other factories. It had become an industrial group with a wide range of products, including audio-visual goods, computer support systems and high-technology video products, as well as owning a number of service, real estate and trading companies. Heavy Electrical too had formed an industrial group after merging with three local factories – one branch factory subsequently entered into a joint venture with a Thai company. Like Audio-Visual it had a number of service companies, plus hotels and restaurants.

The remaining three enterprises were in a different situation. Their sales, but not their work-force, had increased. Pharmaceutical and Electric Switchgear had even cut their staffing level, a result of the municipal government's policy aimed at controlling wages and salaries budgets. As seen in Chapter 5, managers were reluctant to increase employment in order to maintain satisfactory wage levels. Pharmaceutical had completed its investment project in production expansion, but as the health-drink market had become more competitive, the enterprise had had to develop new products to ensure its competitive edge. It had also formed an alliance with a factory in Sichuan in order to enter the local market there. In 1993 Pharmaceutical put forward a radical programme to change its organizational structure. It required its workshops to become independent business units responsible for profit and loss. Three of them formed joint ventures with partners from Japan, Hong Kong and the United States for new product development. The rest of the units engaged in services, supplies, trading, packaging and transport.

Audio's development strategy was similar. Its workshops had become business units, and three joint ventures had been established with partners from Hong Kong, Taiwan and South Korea. Only Electric Switchgear became smaller, because the municipal government had

Table 8.2 Profile of the six enterprises in 1985, 1988 and 1993

Enterprise	Total employment			Sales turnover (Y million)			Net profit before tax (Y million)			Net profit after tax (Y million)			Official size category*			Quota (Q) or profit (P) target		
	1985	1988	1993	1984	1987	1992	1984	1987	1992	1984	1987	1992	1985	1988	1993	1985	1988	1993
Automotive	3883	5100	6000	205	467	1300	53.0	86.0	150.0	6.6	21.1	28.6	M	L	L	Q	Q	P
Audio-Visual	2200	3000	6800	183	418	1070	13.0	13.0	128.0	3.1	4.1	8.4	M	L	L	Q	P	P
Heavy Electrical	1869	1798	2700	23	44	86	4.8	8.6	4.8	0.9	1.7	0.2	M	M	L	Q	P	P
Pharmaceutical	957	912	910	27	43	67	4.0	8.6	4.7	0.8	3.0	0.1	S	M	M	P	P	P
Audio	848	890	900	25	24	60	4.7	0.9	2.5	1.7	0.3	0.6	S	M	M	P	P	P
Electric Switchgear	718	695	630	6	8	16	1.5	2.1	1.3	0.2	0.4	0.2	S	M	M	P	P	P

* L = large, M = medium, S = small. Chinese state-owned enterprises are designated as large, medium or small depending on their output level, value of assets and number of employees.

Sources: Data for 1984, 1985, 1987 and 1988 are from Child and Lu (1990), and MBA project reports at CEMI. Data for 1992 and 1993: interviews held in the enterprises, August 1993.

appropriated some land from its main manufacturing site. This had reduced the enterprise's production capacity, and to compensate the municipal government had lowered the enterprise's contract profit target for three years.

With regard to party organizations, Automotive and Heavy Electrical still retained independent party secretaries. In Audio-Visual and Electric Switchgear the Party secretaries acted as deputy directors, while in Audio and Pharmaceutical the directors acted as party secretaries. The number of salaried Party cadres remained the same as in 1988.

Change in Decision-Making

The method of investigation used in 1993 was very different from the case-study approach of the earlier research. It was derived from the 'Aston Programme' of organizational studies. This involves assessing levels of 47 decision-making activities, focusing particularly on the extent to which decision-making powers are passed down a set of hierarchical levels, both within the enterprise and between the enterprise and a higher authority. Table 8.3 identifies the decision authorization levels in 1993.

In sharp contrast to the two earlier periods, the bureaux' power over enterprise decision making had clearly declined by 1993. Most decisions were taken by managers, and bureau intervention was only found over the introduction of a new cost-budget system. The enterprises had no planning quotas in purchasing and sales. In pricing decisions, all products were in accordance with market prices. Even Automotive and Audio-Visual were free to set market prices.

Regarding labour recruitment and selection, all the enterprises now enjoyed full autonomy, even in the management of senior executives, who were being administered by the director rather than the bureaux. Directors could promote and approve organizational design and change. One important reason for this was that the bureaux had shrunk. Some bureaux, such as the Machine Building Management Bureau and Electronics Industrial Office, had retained some administrative functions in order to coordinate with the enterprises and other government agencies. Each bureau had established business companies. The matrix structure that had connected enterprise departments to the bureaux had been transformed into a relationship between enterprises and the bureaux' companies.

Finally, the enterprises could now decide on new product development, except for strategic investments (see Chapter 7). Investment

Table 8.3 Decision authorization levels in the six enterprises in 1993

Decision activity	Automotive	Audio-Visual	Heavy Electrical	Pharmaceutical	Audio	Electric Switchgear
Purchasing	Deputy director	Deputy director	Deputy director	Purchasing manager	Deputy director	Director
Pricing outputs	Deputy director	Group headquarters	Sales persons	Deputy director	Deputy director	Director
Recruitment	Deputy director	Deputy director	Deputy director	Deputy director	Deputy director	Deputy director
Organizational change	Board	Director	Director	Director	Director	Director
Investment	Board	Group headquarters	Group headquarters[1]	The bureau or director[2]	The bureau or director[2]	The bureau or director[2]
New product development	Board	Group headquarters	Director	Director	Director	Director

Notes:
1. The group headquarters controlled the investment budget. Routine investment was decided by the director.
2. The bureau controlled the investment budget, while the director decided routine investment projects.

Source: Interviews held in the enterprises, August 1993.

proposals depended upon the amount of funding and the nature of the product or industrial sector, and were still controlled by the state. Apart from Audio-Visual, which had continued to invest in innovation and production facilities, most enterprises had not made large investment proposals, but had carried out small investment projects and product development.

While the bureaux had no direct administrative authority, they still had power over three areas. First, the bureaux assessed the enterprises' performances and determined their targets, for instance profit contracts based on the municipal government's new policy. The negotiating relationship between the bureau and the enterprises, which Montias (1988) noted, remained with the CRS. Intensive bargaining and negotiation took place in 1992, when the enterprises renewed their profit contracts. Audio-Visual was allowed to adopt the contractual system for large firms with a favourable scheme of lower interest bank loans and financing autonomy. Heavy Electrical and Pharmaceutical were assigned policies with low taxation and freedom of foreign trade. Electric Switchgear benefited from interest-free loans for its technological innovation. Only Audio failed to meet its contracted profit target in 1991, but instead of penalizing it the bureau decided to lower the profit threshold in the new contract.

Second, the bureau appointed the enterprise director and Party secretary. Although the Workers' Congress was in principle the constitutional body holding such authority, in fact none of the directors had been elected by it. Third, the bureau controlled the strategic activities of the enterprises, such as acquisitions, the formation of joint ventures, exports and cross-regional investment. Both Audio-Visual and Heavy Electrical had sought their bureaux' consent to take over other factories.

Moreover the enterprises relied upon state-controlled institutions such as banks, financial institutions and national distributors, all of which could be affected by state policy. For instance, during July and August 1993 the state imposed an austerity policy to control investment funding and monetary supply – a corrective measure frequently used by the state during the reform (cf. Wu Jinglian, 1993). This immediately led to a shortage of capital as the banks reduced the amount of credit offered to enterprises. More seriously, enterprises such as Heavy Electrical and Electric Switchgear, whose products were sold to industrial customers, were unable to collect their sales credit as buyers had no cash. Automotive's situation was as difficult. In spite of its joint-venture status, both its national distributors and a majority of its customers were controlled by the state. Faced with a shortage of capital, these distributors either cancelled orders or delayed payment. Enterprises such as Audio-Visual, Pharmaceutical and Audio, which produced consumer goods, appeared to fare better because their products went directly to the market through local distributors and private retailers.

The state also intervened via other regulatory authorities. Part of the reason why most enterprises diversified and engaged in a wide range of activities, such as services, so as to absorb employees no longer required on the production lines, was because they were obliged to maintain their staffing level. This was strikingly similar to the situation in 1988 when the RLO scheme was launched by the municipal government. Although official policies granted directors autonomy over labour management, they were not permitted to lay off redundant workers. The local Labour Arbitration Commission reserved the right to review a dismissal decision and could order a firm to reinstate the worker.

Increase of Management Control and New Governance Structure

Apart from the change in the relationship between the enterprises and the bureaux, which had shifted from direct intervention to indirect control, other trends could be identified, namely increased internal control and decreased delegation of authority within the enterprises.

First, after forming a joint venture or an industrial group, the large enterprises established a board of directors (Automotive) or a group headquarters (Audio-Visual and Heavy Electrical). An industrial group included a number of business units for manufacturing, trading, services and functional departments. Consequently management activities became more complex and diversified. This required a board or group headquarters to control and coordinate subordinate factories and functional departments, and to take charge of strategic decision making. The board or group headquarters replaced the bureau in controlling the enterprise and subordinate units. In response to the decline of the bureaux' power, there was a corresponding increase in enterprise centralization. Figure 8.1 shows the governance structure of Audio-Visual in 1993.

Figure 8.1 reveals that the governance structure had changed substantially from the earlier periods when Audio-Visual was a manufacturing unit based on a single site, comprising workshops and functional departments. Now production was only one part of the operation. This new group structure is very similar to the corporate structure of a joint-stock company in a market economy. An enterprise becomes part of a group and follows the group strategy.

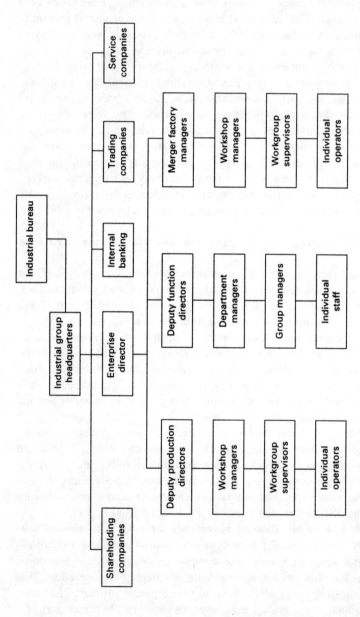

Sources: Interviews and documents held in Audio-Visual, August 1993.

Figure 8.1 Governance structure in the Audio-Visual group, 1993

In contrast with the large enterprise, where the directors were subordinate to boards or headquarters, the smaller enterprises remained as single-site manufacturers with the directors taking all the responsibility under the bureaux' control. Although some enterprises, such as Pharmaceutical and Audio, had many small business units, including joint ventures and service companies, they had not yet developed a group structure. The director had all the power and oversaw all activities.

This trend of centralizing decision making at the board or group headquarters level in large enterprises and at the director level in medium-sized enterprises was a product of the volatile environment. As Mintzberg (1979, pp. 281–82) notes, executives exert more control when the environment is hostile, as the speed and coordination of a centralized response is essential for survival. The year 1993 was a turbulent one for Chinese industry.[15] A severe shortage of working capital and high inflation caused a decline in the performance of many state enterprises. This led to an increase in internal control within the enterprises.

From 1986 onwards an increase in production costs, caused by the inflationary prices of raw materials, threatened the performance of industrial firms. A report drawn up by the MPC pointed out that the realized profit in its 14 industrial bureaux had been reduced from 2.7 billion yuan in 1985 to 1.1 billion yuan in 1989 (Beijing MPC, 1991, p. 74). From 1985 to 1989 the cost of raw materials and energy rose by 87 per cent, employees' salaries by 135 per cent and administrative costs by 151 per cent (ibid., p. 76). A decline in profitability was also evident in the six enterprises. Table 8.4 compares the profits margins and per centages of retained profit in the six enterprise in 1984, 1987 and 1992. In general, in spite of rapid growth in sales in 1992, all but Audio-Visual and Audio experienced a decline in their profit margins. The per centages of retained profits also decreased, in sharp contrast with their increase in 1988.

External pressures from the problematic environment and the decline of economic efficiency pushed senior managers to make most decisions. For instance, purchasing decisions in 1993 were in many cases taken by directors or deputy directors because the state's austerity scheme in July and August caused uncertainties about capital availability. Directors and executives had to control expenditure strictly, especially in purchasing.

As Tisdell (1993) notes, Chinese economic development requires an effective internal disciplinary context, in which managers are able to exert control. With organizational change, particularly in large enterprises, the necessity for an appropriate management control mechanism

Table 8.4 Profit margins and percentage of retained profit in the six
enterprises in 1984, 1987 and 1992

	Profit margin (%) (net profit before tax/sales turnover x 100%)			Percentage of profit retained (net profit after tax/net profit before tax x 100%)		
	1984	*1987*	*1992*	*1984*	*1987*	*1992*
Automotive	25.9	18.4	11.5	12.3	24.5	19.1
Audio-Visual	7.1	3.1	12.0	24.4	31.6	6.5
Heavy Electrical	20.5	19.5	5.6	19.4	19.8	3.1
Pharmaceutical	14.8	19.9	7.0	20.9	35.4	2.8
Audio	18.9	3.8	4.2	37.0	32.7	24.0
Electric Switchgear	24.6	25.3	8.1	13.3	19.9	11.5

Sources: Data for 1984 and 1987: see Table 2.3. Data for 1992: interviews
and documents held in the enterprises, August 1993.

becomes apparent. In Heavy Electrical salespersons determined product prices, and such decisions were commonly made at the lowest levels in all the enterprises. In the 1993 interview the deputy director stated that this power was to be transferred to the director because there had been a sharp decline in profits. In 1991 the Audio-Visual group lost considerable control over its subsidiaries when decision-making was delegated to supervisors and service companies. Therefore in 1992 the group headquarters decided to resume control and an internal banking centre was established to impose cost control measures.

8.4 CONCLUSIONS

Mintzberg (1979) has argued that decentralization within a firm takes place simply because decisions cannot be understood by one person at the top, especially when a firm is growing quickly and its operating sites have become geographically dispersed. Moreover decentralization allows managers at lower levels to respond quickly to the environment (Jennergren, 1981). When decentralization was adopted in China as a national reform policy, it produced mixed results. As this study has shown, through a systematic comparison of the decision-making processes in six enterprises in 1985, 1988 and 1993, decentralization was constrained by the prevailing planning systems, which comprised authorities and governmental agencies.

The decision-making environment in China was characterized by the existence of the planning authorities and a partial market. The state imposed direct control over the enterprises through vertical relations between the enterprises and the bureaux. The bureaux approved strategic and personnel issues, such as the appointment of directors, and assessed enterprise performance. This constraint was derived from state ownership, with the bureaux acting as the representative of the owner. As Nee (1992) notes, state enterprises were constrained by non-market factors in their decision making due to their ownership structure. Child (1994) has shown that even though the relationship between state enterprises and the bureaux had changed from direct administrative intervention to one based on contract, there were still elements in the system that forced enterprises to remain dependent on the bureaux.

Such an institutional framework is not easily removed. The planning authorities control operational resources and personnel. The former includes finance, information, access to the market, strategic materials and human resources. Although the reforms strove to reduce direct administrative intervention by the authorities, indirect intervention was added by the involvement of functional authorities. As Chapter 7 has indicated, investment decisions became more complex and difficult for the enterprises to implement because of the control exerted by numerous authorities and government agencies.

Moreover the market structure, as an economic arena for undertaking transactions, has not yet been sufficiently developed to support the decentralization programme (Solinger, 1989). China's problem is that the market is still underdeveloped and state monopoly artificially suppresses market relations. As Boisot and Child (1995) argue, the Chinese market is a quasi market and relations between enterprises and government agencies are still dominant in economic transactions. This quasi-market was created when the state monopolized the infrastructure, such as resource mobilization, channels of financing and the national distribution network. Thus the state was able to exert an influence on the infrastructure through its policies and regulations, as well as by direct measures such as austerity schemes, which affected enterprises. Mun Kin-Chok (1985) categorized the market structure in China into four groups, namely a directly planned and an indirectly planned market, an enterprise direct sales market and a free market. According to Mun, state enterprises were not in the free market, but mainly in the first three quasi-market forms of the state and market, whilst the non-state enterprises had access to any of the four.

This means that the types of product a firm produces determines the firm's transaction relations with others, such as customers and suppliers.

The closer a firm's products and transaction relations are to the market, the less it is bound by state controls, and managers have more autonomy. Conversely enterprise autonomy is crippled when the infrastructure is dictated by the state. For instance, although Automotive had joint-venture status with complete autonomy in its business dealings, it was still constrained by state-monopolized distribution. In contrast the three enterprises with consumer goods – Audio-Visual, Audio and Pharmaceutical – were closer to the free market.

In such an environment the enterprises responded strategically by developing their organizations through merging with other small factories, investing in suppliers and distributors, as well as subcontracting services to their own companies. These interfirm collaborations were largely used to stabilize transaction relations, as Boisot and Child (1995) have indicated. The unique characteristic of this is the rise of business networks in which government agencies play an active role, and enterprises establish interorganizational relations.

In addition to the problems derived from state ownership and the underdeveloped market infrastructure, there were social–political factors constraining state enterprises. As the case studies have shown, state policies and the underdeveloped social infrastructure constrained the enterprises' pursuit of economic efficiency. Part of this problem could be solved through the development of social welfare systems. But the relationship between management and the Party will be largely dependent upon the progress of the reform of political institutions.

The current reform policies calling for a market economy are plausible, but flawed. This study has shown that a successful reform programme depends upon institutional change. This leads to one of the most complex problems of the reform: the time schedule and the frequency of policy changes. Although it is impossible to transform the system in one giant step, any serious change introduced into an unaltered political and economic environment will be unable to bring about all the desired results. The situation becomes more complex when the actors, for instance enterprise managers and government agencies, act in their own interests.

This study also suggests that Chinese management has some unique cultural features. For instance personal relations (*guanxi*) are used widely in most decision-making processes. As seen in the case studies, interpersonal networks play a crucial role in information communication, bargaining and negotiation, especially when external actors are involved. Although one can argue that such relations exist in other countries, the cases studied here and other research indicate that *guanxi* is particularly favoured by the Chinese in achieving a compromise.[16] As this study has shown, *guanxi* is not only used when dealing with the authorities, but also with other organizations, for instance in purchasing and recruitment. It is obvious that the managers of the six enterprises preferred *guanxi* when seeking opportunities and information for their decisions.

Despite certain limitations, the decentralization programme has positively influenced enterprise management. The enterprise managers gained greater exposure to the market, customers and suppliers since they could no longer rely on the bureaux. One consequence was the acquisition of professional competence and knowledge. With the progress of enterprise autonomy, managerial decision making began to shift from a synoptic approach, in which the process was 'top-down' and normative, to a strategic approach, as Lee (1987) has noted. This strategic decision-making process is driven by market preferences and competitive advantage (cf. Andrew, 1980). As described in the previous section, the enterprises applied various business development strategies, contingent on internal and external contextual variables such as size, product–technology specification and the market situation. In large firms an industrial governance structure was established, based on a corporate group headquarters or the board system, and this governance structure was to some degree similar to that of a joint stock company. Managerial authority was held at a level above the manufacturing units. The rapid growth of both organizational structure and business scope required the establishment of an effective internal discipline mechanism. This in turn prompted a return to centralization, with decision making becoming more concentrated at the board, the headquarters or director level. This indicates the emergence in China of a professional managerial class.

Appendix: Interview Checklist

Q.1 Can you tell me the latest decision taken in one of these areas?
(1) purchase of materials
(2) pricing a product
(3) labour recruitment
(4) organizational change
(5) investment in product development or production processes

Q.2 (With reference to the areas mentioned) when did the decision matter first arise? (month/year)

Q.3 How did it start? (for example: according to market demand, state plans, local government policies, commands from the industrial bureau, or task requirements)

Q.4 Who was involved in the decision process? (Check: organizational chart for internal departments; names of persons, groups, departments and organizations involved)
Who initiated the decision topic? (For example, making proposals)
Who designed the alternatives?
Who selected and evaluated the alternatives?
Who finally authorized the decision?

Q.5 (With reference to the above individuals, groups, departments and organizations) what did each of them initially want in the decision?

Q.6 What did each do in the above process?

Q.7 How much influence did each have?

Q.8 What kind of information did each provide?

Q.9 How was the information used for the decision?

Q.10 When did the decision receive formal approval? And how?

Q.11 How was the decision judged in the process? (For example, according to hard criteria: cost, profit, output values, sales, and wages and bonuses; or soft criteria: reputation, competitive ability, attitude of planning authorities)

Q.12 During the decision-making process were there any interruptions, delays or reconsiderations.

Q.13 Was the same decision taken in 1985? (If no, go to Q. 15)

Q.14 What are the differences between the way such decisions were made in 1985 and this one? (Check: actors involved and their influence, time take and information used. Then, go to Q. 16)

Q.15 If no similar decisions occurred in 1985, when did you first make a decision on the items listed in Q. 1, and what are the differences? (Check: actors involved and their influence, time taken and information used)

Q.16 What are your opinions and comments on the decisions made?

Notes

Introduction

1. The terms 'state planning regime' and 'planning authorities' are used to refer to the institutional agencies that determine priorities, such as state plans for economic activities, and implement these priorities by means of administrative intervention in the operation of enterprises. Their positions of authority over enterprises are legitimised by (1) the control of ownership, for instance of state-owned enterprises, and/or (2) the government apparatus in charge of public interest. These authorities can intervene either directly through assigning quotas in resource allocation or governing an enterprise's specific action, and/or indirectly through issuing policies and regulations.

1 Industrial Governance and Enterprise Management in China, 1949–84

1. China's traditional economy was agrarian (Riskin, 1987), in which bureaucrats performed the essential tasks of coordination, supervision and control of the productive labour of tens of thousands of isolated peasant farms and villages. The production and distribution of goods were substantially limited by this traditional bureaucratic system (Balaze, 1964). In spite of the fact that China created the world's earliest merchandizing industry, there was little change in the level of agricultural production and craft-based manufacturing (c.f. Riskin, 1987). As the early entrepreneurs were inculcated with the values of the scholar–bureaucrat class (Andors, 1977), economic activities were closely linked to the politics and administration of the imperial state. Consequently industrialization did not occur until the last quarter of the ninteenth century, at a time of foreign incursion and internal political upheavals.

   The first attempt to industrialize China took place in the 1860s under the 'self-strengthening' scheme encouraged by the Qing government to strengthen its military forces after China's defeat in two wars – one with Britain (the Opium War of 1842) and one with France (1858–1860) – in addition to internal rebellions. Several industrial projects were modelled on those in Western countries, including the establishment of modern factories. In 1881 China's first telegraph line was completed between Beijing, Tianjin and Shanghai. In 1896 a national postal system was established. Schools started to teach scientific knowledge brought in from Western countries (Beckmann, 1965; Brugger, 1976). This early industrialization was a failure because of several factors – improper government policies, conflicts between Western concepts and Chinese traditional norms, and a lack of qualified political leaders being the main reasons. See Biggerstaff (1976), Brugger (1976), Myers (1982), Xu Dixin (1982), and Zheng Xuemeng *et al.* (1984).

2. Classical socialism occurred first in the former Soviet Union and had the
   following features:

   • An interlocking political–economic state leadership under a hierarchi-
     cally structured Communist Party.
   • A single state-owned complex integrating large economic sectors.
   • A high degree of centralization in planning and control.
   • Ideological motivation and political incentive in management (Spulber,
     1979; Wilczynski, 1972)

3. According to the official definition, the term 'state-owned enterprise' (*guoyou
   qiye*) referred to enterprises 'owned by the whole people' (*quanmin suoyou
   zhi qiye*). They were administered by central or local government. There
   were five sources of state ownership, according to Zhu Jiaming and Lu
   Zheng (1984): (1) firms that were established in the 'Liberated Areas' by
   the Red Army (later the People's Liberation Army) prior to 1949; (2) the
   state taking over the enterprises previously owned by bureaucratic capi-
   talists during the late 1940s; (3) the state nationalizing private industrial
   firms through 'socialist transformation'; (4) the state merging those of
   large collectively owned enterprises; and (5) new firms invested by the
   government.
4. The term 'central planning' refers to a particular mode of administrative
   intervention by central or local government. It is an economic system in
   which (1) the ownership of all or most enterprises is monopolized by the
   state; and (2) the state has the ultimate administrative power to order
   enterprises to accept its objectives, follow its orders with regard to inputs and output and undertake other obligations.
5. For a detailed discussion, see the State Council's Finance and Economic
   System Reform Office (1979), Tian Yuan and Qiao Gang (1991) and Wu
   Jinglian (1992).
6. According to Zhu Jiaming and Lu Zheng (1984) there were four categories of management style among state enterprise, (1) they could be totally
   administered by an industrial ministry, which was usually the case with
   large firms; (2) joint administration by a central ministry and local government, but mainly by the ministry; (3) joint administration by a ministry
   and local government, but mainly by the local authority; and (4) total
   control by the local government. The number of state enterprises subject
   to each of the categories varied at different times. For example by 1980
   2500 state firms, that is, approximately 3 per cent of industrial firms,
   were subject to central government control, while the rest were managed
   by local governments.
7. This was seen as dramatically different from the former Soviet Union's
   'one-man management model'. Donnithorne (1967) describes managerial
   human resources in the early 1950s. Andors (1977) provides a more detailed description of the establishment of the collective leadership in China,
   with the Party as the supreme authority.
8. This was in the speech Ma Hong delivered to the Shanxi Provincial Party
   Committee on 17 August 1979.
9. For a detailed discussion of attempts at decentralization prior to 1978,

see Donnithorne (1967), Lee (1987), Zhu Jiaming and Lu Zheng (1984), Riskin (1987), and Wu Jinglian (1992).

10. Wu Jinglian (1989) argues that it was common for an economic measure or even an idea to be linked to ideological concepts. Thus a reform policy was considered for political reasons rather than economic ones.

11. Fei Xiaotong (1967, p. 37) states, 'In this society, a universal standard did not work. [An actor] must ask clearly who was the subject and what kind of relationship he enjoys with the subject; he then decides what kind of standards to make his judgement'.

12. See Zhou Enlai (1975).

2 Economic Reform: Decentralization 1984–88

1. See State Council's Finance and Economic System Reform Office (1979), pp. 826–4.

2. See CPC (Communist Party of China) (1984).

3. For further details regarding the DRS, the CRS and the reform of state enterprises from 1979 to 1988, see Former Enterprise Bureau of the SEC (1988), Xu Feiqing and Wang Shengrui (1993), Chapter 6, and Wu Zhenkun and Chen Wentong (1993), Chapters 7 and 8.

4. The decision was taken at a conference organized by the SEC, the Organization Ministry of the Central Party Committee and the National Federation of Trade Unions in August 1987.

5. There were five main forms of the CRS: (1) 'two guarantees and one link', mostly around Beijing (see Chapter 2.3), (2) profit growth contract, (3) profit annual lump sum contract, (4) profit target contract or subsidy contract for loss-making industries and (5) input–output contracts in large firms. See the Former Enterprise Bureau of the SEC (1988) and Byrd (1988).

6. See Chapter 8 for further details.

7. Wu Jinglian (1988) noted that it was not unusual during the period of reform for Chinese academics to be sceptical of Western economic theories based on the market economy. Wu also pointed out that theories were categorized according to views from the top. His proposal of 'integrated design' was criticized as 'politically conservative' and 'anti-reformist'. A later example can be found in the CRS design. Official propaganda described it as 'a milestone in China's reform progress', or 'a management system with Chinese characteristics'. See 'Summary of Opinions on the CRS' (1988) and the *Beijing Daily*'s report on Li Peng's speech during the Chinese New Year when he visited the Shougang (*Beijing Daily*, 4 April 1988).

8. See Chen Fengying (1989) and Liu Moshan (1989). Both Chen and Liu identified similar problems in the CRS. These included bargaining to lower their profit target; more bonus allocation than contracted and no penalty if the contract terms were not met.

9. A typical example was reported by the *Economic Daily* (10 February 1989, p. 1). An enterprise director stated: 'According to the decentralization programme, the state government has delegated certain powers, such as autonomy of personnel, organizational design, but I have not yet

received these. Or, more accurately, I have not yet received all of them. I find it difficult to identify who or which agent stopped the decentralization. What I can say is that the central government is too high at the top of the hierarchy, and we are at the bottom.... So that the autonomy delegated from the top has not reached the enterprises'. See also Yuan Baohua's speech to the Economic Committee of the National Political Consultative Conference (Yuan Baohua, 1989b).

10. See Chapter 4 for further details.
11. Zhu Rongji was the then vice chairman of the SEC.
12. Battat (1986, p. 70) noted: 'To convince others and provide themselves with the necessary ideological security and legitimacy, management advocates called upon Marx, Lenin and Mao, selectively quoting them at length to prove their support for the use of modern management in developing a socialist economy. In these advocates' views, as long as it fits China's situation and socialism, modern management should be used, whether developed in China or imported from abroad and adapted to the national needs'.
13. 'Corresponding management' means that departments in government agencies and in enterprises have similar functions and a formal relationship. The enterprises are required to carry out specific tasks on the orders of the agencies. For example, regarding quality control, both the industrial bureau and the enterprise have a quality control office. The head of the enterprise office must report to and meet the head of the bureau office and follow the instruction given by the bureau's office. See Chapter 6 for further details.
14. These three firms were Shougang, the Beijing Internal-Combustion Engine Factory and the Beijing Qinghe Woollen Fibre Mill.
15. Interview at the municipal government, October 1988.
16. Interviews and documents at the enterprises, August–October 1988.
17. The other reason was the failure of the reform of the taxation system. *Beijing Daily*, 7 November, 1988, p. 1.
18. Interviews and documents at the enterprises, August–October 1988.
19. Interviews and documents, the municipal government, October 1988.
20. In some enterprises, such as Audio-Visual, Automotive and Heavy Electrical, the appointment of senior executives before 1988 needed the approval of the bureaux.

3 Purchase Decision-Making: Raw Materials

1. The division of goods in China also followed the definition of their use. Therefore there were *production materials* (*shengchan ziliao*) and *consumer goods* (*xiaofei ziliao*). The production materials were monopolized by the State Bureau for the Supply of Raw Materials, industrial ministries and local governments. Consumer goods were distributed by the state commerce system, in which the Ministry of Commerce had authority over local commerce bureaux.
2. Wang Dayong (1989, p. 16) argues that the implementation of the CRS pushed managers to increase stocks of materials or product prices to protect profitability. Both led to inflation.

3. Data from 'Change and influence of the industrial production expenses' (*gongye shengchan feiyong de bianhua ji yingxiang*), Beijing Municipal Finance & Administration Research Institute. It is included in Beijing MPC, *Integrative Economic Study* (*zonghe jingji yanjiu*) (Beijing: Beijing Science & Technology Press, 1991), pp. 74–81.

4 Price Decision-Making: Economic Motives and Societal Constraints

1. There were several attempts to reform the price system in China prior to 1978. Sun Yefang was the first economist to propose that the law of value be used as a guideline in plan making, which meant introducing price as a lever in resource allocation and a determinant of values in product exchange. In the early 1960s Sun Yefang proposed using the law of value as a measure of enterprise performance according to economic indicators, including cost, prices, productivity and so on. However, these arguments were dismissed. See Riskin (1987, pp. 158–69); Sun Yefang (1980); Wu Jinglian (1992).
2. See the State Council's Finance and Economic System Reform Office (1979). This document was a proposal for the State Council's policy of the economic reform.
3. See Diao Xinsheng (1987) and the State Council's Finance and Economic System Reform Office (1979). The concept of the dual price system originated in the 1979 proposal. But it was not officially determined as the main programme in price reform until 20 October 1984 at the Third Plenum of the 12 Central Committee of the CPC. The CPC's decision on economic structure reform emphasized the reduction of state prices and delegation of appropriate price-setting autonomy to the local government and enterprises.
4. Tian Yuan and Qiao Gang (1991) examined the price reform from 1978 to 1990 through systematic analyses of the reform designs, problems and statistics. They noted that from 1986 to 1988 panic buying was found in different regions.
5. Tian Yuan and Qiao Gang (1991) investigated 281 enterprises in 1986 across 14 districts. They found that most enterprises transferred their cost increases to prices.
6. The Beijing municipal government issued a regulation on 28 February 1989 to recentralize price approval: interviews and documents at the enterprises and the Beijing municipal government, May 1989.
7. In a specific case, industrial ministries could send observers to large steel firms. This was the action taken by the government in 1988 for the purpose of controlling steel prices.
8. The term 'market mechanism' here refers to the institutional setting in which the exchange of products and services was determined by direct negotiation between supplier and buyer, neither having authority over the other.
9. Reports submitted by a state enterprise to its authority was hardly recognized as an internal document, because internal documents in China referred only to those written documents distributed by the state, and usually among units above the bureau level.

10. Oksenberg (1974) noted that the communication system within Chinese bureaucracy was loosely integrated and there existed a complex set of channels that were used at a different stage in the policy process. It relied on verbal communication and secrecy, and was vertically directed. Communication between those at the lower levels and the top was not efficient, and local bureaux had their own distinctive blend of communication depending on the tasks and technologies available to them.

11. The shortage of colour TVs was caused by the shortage of imported components, because most colour TV lines were licensed by foreign companies.

12. This became illegal after the Anti-unfair Competition Law came into force in 1993.

5 Recruitment Decisions

1. For a detailed study, see Zhao Lukuan and Lu Guotai (1992) and Xia Jizhi and Dang Xiaojie (1991).

2. In 1956 a Chinese delegation visited the former Soviet Union. A proposal to adopt a 'contract labour system' was later forwarded to the government. See Li Boyong (1987).

3. Li Boyong (1987) has reviewed the development of contract labour systems in China since the 1950s and 1960s.

4. The World Bank (1985, p. 131) notes: 'These and other reforms, though beneficial, have not basically changed the system. The unified assignment scheme is still used for virtually all those with any post-secondary training and for some skilled manual workers. Enterprises can seldom hire badly needed skilled workers from other enterprises where their skills may be less valuable; they are still obliged by the labour bureaux to accept "packages" containing both wanted and unwanted recruits; they cannot discharge redundant workers; and they have been allowed to dismiss unsatisfactory workers only in a few instances, involving extreme absenteeism or malfeasance. It appears imperative to consider further, more radical changes'.

5. For further details, see Zhang Xiaojian *et al.* (1991)

6. Walder (1986) noted that enterprises in China were like traditional communities, integrating economic, social and political obligations to their employees.

6 Organizational Change: The Relationship between Management and the Communist Party

1. See Chinese Economic Operation Research Project Team (1988). It notes that state enterprises have three obligations, namely economic performance, political tasks and social welfare facilities.

2. See Table 2. 6, which shows that most directors were appointed during 1984 and 1986, when the change was initiated.

3. Riskin (1987, pp. 83–4) states: 'By the phrase "politicization of economic decision-making", I mean three things: first, the extensive use of general criteria of choice (e.g., that industry should support agriculture, that each locality should strive to build up a comprehensive and relatively independent industrial system, that rural incomes should be distributed

basically according to work done and secondarily on a per capita "supply" basis, etc.) that were passed down from the central party and government organs as general directives; second, the fact that these and other guidelines for choice were often expressed in slogan form ("walk on two legs", "go all out, aim high, strive to build socialism more, faster, better, and more economically", "both read and expert", "get going with local methods", etc.); and third, the fact that ideological values came to be substituted for objective engineering or economic standards of choice'.

4. See Beijing MEC (1988). This was the MEC's summary report of the RLO.

5. See Gong Shuji (1989). Gong Shuji was then chief of the Municipal Labour Bureau. This was his summary report of the RLO.

6. See Department of Enterprise Management of the SCRES (1989). It reported that workers were influenced by the traditional concepts of socialism, which had argued that 'unemployment is a product of capitalism, and that there should be no unemployment in a socialist country. Dismissing a worker therefore conflicts with the principles of socialism; that workers are the master class in enterprises, and they have the right and responsibility to work there. Removing redundant workers from production positions is seen to violate workers' rights'. The report found that 'these concepts encouraged some redundant workers to rebel and complain after they were laid off from production positions; they also made some managers afraid of making political mistakes. As a result, managers did not implement the scheme, but waited for a change in policies'.

7. These included 154 from the industrial bureau, 29 from the municipal government, 26 from the Ministry of Electronics, five from the MEC, four from the MPC, and 23 from various associations, the ministry's companies and the bureau.

8. These included 243 from the industrial bureau, 80 from the state/municipal governments and ministries and 20 from other organizations.

9. Li Ximing's speech at the working conference in July 1988 (quoted in Gong Shuji, 1989, pp. 3–4). Li Ximing was then secretary of the municipal Party committee.

10. Chamberlain (1987) provides a more detailed discussion of the relationship between Party secretaries and directors.

7 Investment Decision-Making: Product and Production Innovation

1. Here the discussion is limited to direct investment, rather than portfolio investment and investment in stock and security markets.

2. This policy is called 'grants replaced by loans' (*buo gai dai*). It was first attempted as an experiment in 1979, and then introduced on a large scale in 1982. From 1979 to 1987 bank loans accounted for 35.2 per cent of total investment capital. See Department of Institutional and Legal Reform in the SPC (1988).

3. The reform of depreciation started in 1978, when the government permitted enterprises to retain 50 per cent of depreciation. In 1979, this was increased to 100 per cent. However in 1985 the regulation changed slightly and enterprises were allowed to keep 70 per cent, leaving the remaining

30 per cent to be managed by the industrial bureaux. This was again amended in 1987, and enterprises were permitted to keep 100 per cent of depreciation. See the Ministry of Finance (1988).
4. See Zhong Chengxun (1993). Zhong and his colleagues argue that the decentralization of investment decision making in 1984 failed to delegate autonomy to enterprises. Most decision-making powers were hijacked by the local governments. Furthermore in 1989 the State Council published a policy regarding national industrial development. The policy categorized industrial sectors and products into three groups: strategic, non-strategic and restricted. The government encouraged investment in strategic ones, allowed local governments and/or firms to finance the non-strategic, but intervened in investments in restricted industries.
5. Zhong Chengxun (1993) argues that local governments were motivated to have more investment projects and more autonomy in deciding investments, because investment contributed to local economic development and increased employment. In the pursuit of local interest, local governments became involved in enterprise investment and lobbied the central government to increase investment budgets.
6. See the Department of Comprehensive Planning of the SCESR (1988).
7. Zhong Chengxun (1993) notes that local governments were motivated to increase investment projects in accordance with local economic interests. Thus many projects were duplicated across provinces and municipalities.
8. See *China's investment white paper 1993*, pp. 117–27. More than 70 per cent of sample enterprises with investments believed that it was difficult to assert their autonomy in investment decision making, and about 37 per cent complained that they had no power to determine the size of their investments.
9. See *China's Investment White Paper 1993*. It was noted that control of industrial structure and investment was mainly held by the central government, while local government had a strong influence.

8 Summary, Current Reform of State Enterprises and Conclusions

1. Hickson and his colleagues compared 150 decisions in 30 organizations and found that organizational change and technological innovation usually took longer and were complex in actor involvement. Yuan Lu and Heard (1995) compared strategic investment decision processes in China and the UK and found that both were lengthy and complex, involving many actors from inside and outside the firms.
2. See *China Reform and Development Report: 1992–1993*, pp. 32–3. It is noted that the decentralization programme neither created a market environment nor improved the performance of state enterprises. For instance state enterprises and local government agencies with more freedom were motivated to increase their investments and expenditure on welfare, and there was a lack of an effective discipline mechanism to control and supervise behaviour. See also *The Voice of Productive Forces* (1993), where it was reported that industrial enterprises in Beijing suffered from a fall in retained profits from January to September 1993. The main reason was a shortage of working capital.

3. See Wu Zhenkun and Chen Wentong (1993), who reported that 90 per cent of state enterprises in 1993 adopted the CRS. They argued that there were, at least in the near future, few alternatives to the CRS.
4. See Wu Zhenkun and Chen Wentong (1993, pp. 130–1), who note that it was difficult to have an effective contract system because the profit contract was usually a result of negotiation. Furthermore the CRS encouraged the short-term behaviour (three to four years) and failed to motivate the enterprises to focus on long-term development.
5. On 23 May 1990 the State Council forwarded the proposal of the SCRES to strengthen enterprise reform. It emphasized improving the CRS by carrying out technological innovation.
6. Wu Zhenkun and Chen Wentong (1993, pp. 132–9) note that many local government agencies hijacked decision-making autonomy from enterprises.
7. Song Maoguang (1993) identified four phases of market understanding in China. The first was in the early 1980s, when most economists in China viewed the market as a place where commodities were exchanged. The second was during mid-1980s, when people started to realize that the market was a set of exchange relations that governed transaction behaviour. The third was in the late 1980s when, led by Wu Jinglian and his colleagues, the market was regarded as a mechanism with its own rules and processes. The fourth started after Deng Xiaoping's 1992 southern China tour, when state policies viewed the markets as an economic mechanism. Song noted that during 1989 and 1991 many economists opposed the market and equated a market economy with capitalism. This was largely caused by the political climate after 1989. See also *Beijing Review*, no. 15, 1992, 'Deng Xiaoping maps out bolder reform'.
8. See Department of Administration of the China Central Party University (1993), a collection articles by a number of high-ranking officials and economists.
9. There is ambiguity in the definition of the operating mechanism. The reform policy for the 1990s called for the establishment of modern enterprise governance, meaning the shareholder committee, the board of directors and the supervisory board. It also emphasized the role of the Party committee and the Workers' Congress. See Modern Enterprise Institutional Investigation Team (1993).
10. See the *People's Daily* (overseas edition), 8 February 1995, p. 1, 'The State Economic and Trade Commission announced the key issues relating to the reform of state enterprises in this year' (*guojia jingmao wei gongbu guoyou qiye jinnian gaige yaodian*). It was stated that the reform focused on the experience of modern enterprise institutions, implementation of the enterprise law and the State Council's policy of transforming the operating mechanism, the acceleration of technological innovation, the treatment of redundant workers, enterprise bankruptcy, bad debts, internal management, the industrial structure and industrial groups. See also *China Reform and Development Report: 1992–1993*, pp. 33–7. The report argued that decentralization was limited by the ownership structure. It proposed that state ownership be represented by an independent entity, rather than industrial bureaux or ministries.

11. Reported in *The Voice of Productive Forces* (*shengchan li zhisheng*), 1994, no. 5, pp. 19–21.
12. See MacMurray and Woetzel (1994), who note that state enterprises had a labour cost disadvantage because they had to provide retirement benefits, social benefits and pension allowances.
13. On 29 February 1993 the Beijing municipal government published its policy on transforming the operating mechanism of state enterprises. It confirmed the 14 decisions where enterprises could exercise autonomy and delegated powers of mergers and acquisitions to enterprise management. See *Collection of measures regarding the transformation of the operating mechanisms in enterprises owned by all the people* (1993).
14. The investigation in 1993 was jointly conducted by Yuan Lu and John Child.
15. *China Reform and Development Report: 1992–1993* noted that the chaos in the economic environment was caused by overheated industrial growth, which started the inflation and brought about a money supply shortage.
16. See Yuan Lu and Heard (1995), who found that personal relations in China are extensively used to facilitate formal procedures and amend the decision rationale, for instance the rate of return in investment. In the UK such relations have been used to increase trust, but have rarely changed formal procedures and rationale.

References

Andors, S. (1977) *China's industrial revolution* (London: Martin Robertson).

Andrew, K. R. (1980) *The concept of corporate strategy*, revised edition (Ontario: Richard D. Irwin).

Balaze, Etienne (1964) *Chinese civilization and bureaucracy* (New York: Yale University Press).

Barnowe, J. Thad. (1990) 'Paradox resolution in Chinese attempts to reform organizational culture', in John Child and Martin Lockett (eds), *Advances in Chinese Industrial Studies*, vol. 1, *Reform Policy and the Chinese Enterprise* (London: JAI Press), pp. 329–49.

Bate, Paul and John Child (1987) 'Paradigms and understandings in comparative organizational research', in John Child and Paul Bate (eds), *Organization of innovation: East–West perspectives* (Berlin: Walter de Gruyter), pp. 19–49.

Battat, Joseph (1986) *Management in post-Mao China* (Michigan: UMI Research Press).

Beckmann, G. M. (1965) *The modernization of China and Japan* (New York: Harper & Row).

Beijing Daily, 4 April 1988, p. 3, 'Creating a state-owned large enterprise with Chinese characteristics' (*suzao you zhongguo tese de quanmin da qiye*). This was Li Peng's speech in the 1988 Spring Festival when he visited Shougang.

Beijing Daily, 14 August 1988, p. 1, 'The breakthrough in the deepening enterprise reform' (*zhuazhu le shenhua qiye gaige de tupuo kou*).

Beijing Daily, 7 November 1988, p. 3. 'Current choice of industrial enterprise reform and its performance' (*gongye qiye gaige de xianshi xuanze ji chengxiao*).

Beijing MEC (1988) 'Realizing Rationalizing Labour Organization, deepening enterprise internal reform' (*shixing laodong youhua zuhe, shenjua qiye neibu gaige*), in Beijing Municipal Economic Commission (ed.), *Prospect is in Rationalizing* (*xiwang zai youhua*) (Beijing: Beijing Daily Press), pp. 20–28.

Beijing MPC (1991) 'Analysis of Beijing municipal industrial economic performance' (*Beijing shi gongye jingji xiaoyi fenxi*), in Beijing MPC (ed.), *General economic research* (*zonghe jingji yanju*) (Beijing: Beijing Science and Technology Press), pp. 48–65.

Beijing Review, no. 5 (1988), 'Attitude survey of city dwellers', pp. 24–8.

Beijing Review, no. 15 (1992), 'Deng Xiaoping maps out bolder reform', p. 6.

Beijing Review, no. 24 (1992), 'Enterprise reform: new operating mechanism', pp. 14–20.

Beijing Review, no. 42 (1992), 'Party Congress introduces market economy', pp. 5–6.

Beijing Review, no. 46 (1992), 'State-owned enterprises no longer state run', pp. 13–17.

Berger, Peter L. (1986) *The capitalist revolution* (Aldershot: Gower).

Biggerstaff, K. C. (1976) 'Modernization and early modern China', in E. E. Black (ed.), *Comparative modernization* (New York: The Free Press), pp. 146–64.

Blecher, M. (1989) 'State administration and economic reform', in David Goodman and Gerald Segal (eds), *China at forty: Mid-life crisis?* (Oxford: Oxford University Press), pp. 18–41.

Boisot, Max and John Child (1995) 'China's emerging economic order: modernization through network quasi-capitalism?', unpublished paper, Judge Institute of Management Studies, University of Cambridge, Cambridge.

Bower, Joseph L. (1970) *Managing the resource allocation process* (Boston, MA: Division of Research, Harvard Business School).

Brugger, W. (1976) *Democracy & organization in Chinese industrial enterprises: 1948–1953* (Cambridge: Cambridge University Press).

Butler, R. (1991) *Designing organizations* (London: Routledge).

Butler, R., L. Davies, R. Pike and J. Sharp (1993) *Strategic investment decisions* (London: Routledge).

Byrd, William A. (1987) 'The role and impact of markets', in Gene Tidrick and Chen Jiyuan (eds), *China's industrial reform* (Oxford: Oxford University Press for the World Bank).

Byrd, William A. (1988) 'Contractual responsibility systems in Chinese state-owned industry: A preliminary assessment', paper presented at the International Conference on Management in China Today, 20–21 June, Leuven, Belgium.

Byrd, William A. (ed.) (1992) *Chinese industrial firms under reform* (Oxford: Oxford University Press for the World Bank).

Campbell, Robert (1966) 'On the theory of economic administration', in Henry Rosovsky (ed.), *Industrialization in Two systems* (New York: John Wiley & Sons), pp. 186–203.

Chamberlain, Heath B. (1987) 'Party–management relations in Chinese industries: some political dimensions of economic reform', *China Quarterly*, no. 112, pp. 632–61.

Chen Fengying (1989) 'Strengthening audit and supervision, improving enterprise CRS' (*jiaqiang shenji jiandu wanshan qiye chengbao zhi*), in *Enterprise Management Reference* (*qiye guanli cankao*), 17 August (Beijing: China Enterprise Management Association), pp. 18–21.

Chen Xitong (1988) Speech at the Municipal Industrial Work Conference (*shi gongye gongzuo huiyi shang de jianghua*), 16 July, 1988, in Gong Shuji (ed.), *Practice of the RLO* (*youhua laodong zuhe shijian*) (Beijing: Science and Technology Press), pp. 5–6.

Child, John (1987) 'Enterprise reform in China: problems and progress', in M. Warner (ed.), *Management reforms in China* (London: Frances Pinter), pp. 24–52.

Child, John (1994) *Management in China during the age of reform* (Cambridge: Cambridge University Press).

Child, John and Yuan Lu (1990) 'Industrial decision-making under China's reform: 1985–1988', *Organization Studies*, vol. 11, no. 3, pp. 321–51.

China Enterprise Management Association (1989) 'Report on policy of activating large and medium sized backbone enterprises' (*guanyu gaohuo dazhong xing gugan qiye youguan zhengce de baogao*), unpublished report, October (Beijing: China Enterprise Management Association).

China People's Bank (1988) 'Reforming the financial system, strengthening macro-management' (*gaige jinrong tizhi jiaqiang hongguan guanli*), in SCRES (State Commission for Restructuring Economic Systems) (ed.) *Ten years of China's economic systems reform* (*zhongguo jingjitizhi gaige shinian*) (Beijing: Economic Management Press and Reform Press), pp. 503–13.

China Reform and Development Report 1992–1993 (*zhongguo gaige yu fazhan baogao 1992–1993*) (Beijing: China Finance and Economic Press).

China's Investment White Paper 1993 (1993 *zhongguo touzi baipi shu*), edited by Investment Research Institute of the SPC and State Statistical Bureau (Beijing: China Planning Press).

China Statistical Yearbook 1992 (Beijing: China Statistical Press).

Chinese Economic Operation Research Project Team (1988) 'Enterprises' three-in-one functions in our country' (*woguo qiye de sanwei yiti xingzhi*), *Guangming Daily*, 8 August, p. 3.

Collection of measures regarding the transformation of the operating mechanisms in industrial enterprises owned by all the people (*quan min suoyou zhi gongye qiye zhuanhuan jingying jizhi shishi banfa huibian*), edited by the Department of Policy and Regulation in the SCRES, the Department of Enterprises in the State Economic and Trade Commission and Law Bureau of the State Council (Beijing: China Economic Press, 1993).

CPC (Communist Party of China) (1984) *China's economic structure reform: decision of the CPC Central Committee* (Beijing: Foreign Languages Press).

Dang Xiaojie, Wang Aiwen and Tu Dianping (1991) 'Reform of our country's labour institutions' (*woguo laodong tizhi gaige*), in Xia Jizhi and Dang Xiaojie (eds) *Employment and unemployment in China* (*zhongguo de jiuye yu shiye*) (Beijing: China Labour Press), pp. 191–219.

Deng Xiaoping (1985) speech at the National Conference of the Communist Party of China, 23 September 1985, *EBIS*, Daily Report: China, 23 September, K8–13, quoted from Christopher M. Clarke (1986, p. 120), 'Rejuvenation, reorganization and the dilemmas of modernization in post-Deng China', *Journal of International Affairs*, vol. 39, no. 2, pp. 119–32.

Department of Administration of the China Central Party University (ed.) (1993) *Authoritative people discussing the transformation from a planned economy to a market one* (*quan wei renshi tan cong jihua jingji zhuan xiang shichang jingji*) (Beijing: The China Central Party University Press).

Department of Comprehensive Planning of the SCRES (1988) 'Reform of the macro-economic administration', (*hongguan jijing guanli de gaige*), in SCRES (ed.), *Ten years of China's economic systems reform* (Beijing: Economic Management Press and Reform Press), pp. 479–84.

Department of Enterprise Management of the SCRES (1989) 'The current contradictions and problems in Rationalizing labour organization and their solutions', in *Economic Management* (*jingji guanli*), no. 2, quoted from the *New China Monthly Report* (*xihua yuebao*), vol. 3, 1989, pp. 71–2.

Department of Institutional and Legal Reform of the SPC (1988) 'The reform of the planning system' (*jihua tizhi de gaige*), in SCRES (ed.), *Ten years of China's economic systems reform* (*zhongguo jingji gaige shinian*) (Beijing: Economic Management Press and Reform Press), pp. 485–502.

Diao Xinsheng (1987) 'The role of the two-tier price system', in Bruce L. Reynolds (ed.), *Reform in China: challenges & choices* (New York: M. E. Sharpe), pp. 35–46.

Donnithorne, A. (1967) *China's economic system* (London: George Allen and Unwin).

Economic Daily, 14 November, 1988, p. 1, 'Why control over investment has been lost' (*weishenme touzi shikong*).

Economic Daily, 20 December, 1988, p. 1, 'The State Council's examination groups will go to local areas again' (*guowuyuan jiancha zhu jiang zaifu ge di*).

Economic Daily, 10 February, 1989, p. 1, 'What is most needed for enterprises' (*qiye zuixuyao shenme*).

Economic Reference (*jingji cankao*), 17 November 1989, p. 1, 'Remedy for macro and micro environments does not stop enterprise reform' (*daxiao huanjing yiqi zhi qiye gaige bu tingbu*).

Fan Qimiao (1989) 'Compendium of literature on price and price reform in China', *China Programme Working Paper*, no. 2 (London: London School of Economics).

Fang Sheng (1992) 'Opening up and making use of capitalism', *Beijing Review*, no. 12, pp. 17–19.

Fei Xiaotong (1967) *China* (*xiangtu zhongguo*) (Taibei: Green Continental Press).

Former Enterprise Bureau of the SEC (1988) 'Revitalising enterprises as the central task, continuing to deepen the enterprise reform' (*yi gaohuo qiye wei zhongxin, bu duan shen hua qiye gaige*), in SCRES (ed.), *Ten years of China's economic systems reform* (*zhongguo jingji tizhi gaige shinian*) (Beijing: Economic Management Press and Reform Press), pp. 229–39.

Gao Xuechun, Wen Wei and Chen Jing (1989) 'Directors' answers to a questionnaire on deepening enterprise reform' (*changzhang dui shenhua qiye gaige wenjuan de huida*). *Enterprise Management Reference* (*qiye guanli cankao*), 21 August 1989, pp. 2–6.

Gong Shuji (1989) 'The basic condition of the RLO in Beijing' (*Beijing shi laodong yuhua zuhe gongzou de jiben qingkuang*), in Gong Shuji (ed.), *Practice of the RLO* (*laodong youhua zuhe shijian*) (Beijing: Science & Technology Press), pp. 35–51.

Granick, David (1990) *Chinese state enterprises* (Chicago: University of Chicago Press).

Greiner, Larry (1970) 'Patterns of organization change', in Gene Dalton, Paul Lawrence and Larry Greiner (eds), *Organizational change and development* (Homewood, Illinois: The Dorsey Press), pp. 213–29.

Guangming Daily, 11 February 1988, p. 1, 'Directors from 51 large enterprises put forward nine proposals regarding revitalising large enterprises' (*wushiyi jia daqiye fuzeren tichu gaohuo da qiye de jiutiao jianyi*).

Hickson, D. J., R. Butler, D. Cray, G. Mallory, and D. Wilson (1986) *Top decisions: strategic decision making in organizations* (Oxford: Basil Blackwell).

Hofstede, G. (1980) *Culture's consequence: international differences in work-related values* (Beverly Hills, Calif.: Sage).

Hu, H. C. (1944) 'The Chinese concepts of face', *American Anthropologist*, vol. 46, pp. 45–63.

Huang Xiaojing and Yang Xiao (1987) 'From Iron Rice Bowls to Labour Markets: Reforming the Social Security System', in B. L. Reynolds (ed.), *Reform in China: challenges & choices* (New York: M. E. Sharpe), pp. 147–60.

Hussain, Athar (1990) *The Chinese enterprise reforms*, programme of research into the reform of pricing and market structure in China, STICERD (London: London School of Economics).

Hwang, K. K. (1983) 'Face and favour: Chinese power games', unpublished manuscript, National Taiwan University, quoted in M. Bond and K. K. Hwang (1986), *The Psychology of the Chinese People* (Hong Kong: Oxford University Press), pp. 223–4.

Jacobs, J. B. (1979) 'A preliminary model of particularistic ties in Chinese political alliances: Kan-ch'ing and kuan-hsi in a rural Taiwanese township', *China Quarterly*, no. 78, pp. 232–73.

Jennergren, L. Peter (1981) 'Decentralization in organization', in Paul C. Nystrom and William H. Starbuck (eds), *Handbook of Organization Design*, vol. 2, pp. 39–59 (Oxford: Oxford University Press).

Ji Zongwen (1988) 'Review and prospect of reforming planning systems in Beijing Municipality' (*Beijing shi jihua tizhi gaige de huigu yu qianzhan*), *Capital Economy* (*shoudu jingji*), vol. 2, pp. 7–11.

Kerr, C. (1983) *The future of industrial societies* (Cambridge, MA: Harvard University Press).

Kerr, C., J. T. Dunlop, F. H. Harbison and C. A. Myers (1960) *Industrialism and Industrial Man* (Harmondsworth: Penguin, 1973).

King, Paul (1975) 'Is the emphasis of capital budgeting theory misplaced?', *Journal of Business Finance and Accounting*, vol. 2, no. 1, pp. 69–82.

Kornai, Janos (1980) *The Economics of Shortage* (Amsterdam: North-Holland).

Kornai, Janos (1986) 'The Hungarian reform process: visions, hopes and reality', *Journal of Economic Literature*, vol. 24, pp. 1687–737.

Kornai, Janos (1989) 'Some lessons from the Hungarian experience for Chinese reformers', in Peter Van Ness (ed.), *Market reforms in socialist societies* (London: Lynne Rienner), pp. 75–104.

Laaksonen, Oiva (1988) *Management in China during and after Mao in enterprises, government and Party* (Berlin: Walter de Gruyter).

Lee, Hong Yung (1986) 'The implications of reform for ideology, state and society in China', *Journal of International Affairs*, vol. 39, no. 2, pp. 77–90.

Lee, Peter (1987) *Industrial management and economic reform in China: 1949–84* (Oxford: Oxford University Press).

Li Boyong (1987) Speech at the national conference on activating permanent employment systems, in Gong Shuji (ed.), *Practice of the RLO* (*youhua laodong zuhe shijian*) (Beijing: Science and Technology Press, 1989), pp. 19–31.

Li Guang-an (1988) 'China's planning management and planning systems reform' (*zhongguo jihua tizhi guanli he jihua tizhi gaige*), in *Study Materials for Economists* (*jingji gongzuozhe xuexi cailiao*), vol. 21, pp. 30–5.

Li Lianzhong (1987) 'Chaotic behaviour of enterprises and the remedy approach during a period of institutional transition' (*tizhi zhuangui shiqi de qiye xingwei wenluan yu zhili*), in *Exploration of Systems Reform* (*jingji tizhi gaige tansuo*), vol. 1, pp. 45–50.

Li Peilin, Jiang Xiaoxing and Zhang Qizai (1992) *Chinese enterprises in transformation* (*zhuan xing zhong de zhongguo qiye*) (Jinan: Shandong People's Press).

Li Peng (1988) speech at the national planning and economic systems reform conference on 5 December 1988, *Quishi* (1989), vol. 1, pp. 4–9.

Li Ximing (1989) Speech at the work conference, July 1988, in Gong Shuji (ed.), *Practice of the RLO* (*youhua laodong zuhe shijian*) (Beijing: Science and Technology Press), pp. 3–4.

Lian He (1988) 'Before and after the Enterprise Law' (*qiyefa quian quian hou hou*), *Modern Enterprise* (*xiandai qiye daokan*), vol. 4, pp. 5–7.

Lin Zili (1980) 'The beginning of economic systems reform in our country' (*woguo jingji tizhi gaige de kaiduan*), in *Collection of Economic Essays 1980* (*jingji xue wenji 1980*) (Hangzhou: Zhejiang People's Press), pp. 209–234.

Liu Guoguang (1988) 'Review of China's economic reform theories in last ten years' (*zhongguo jingji gaige lilun shinian huigu*), in SCRES (ed.), *Ten years of China's economic systems reform* (*Zhongguo jingji tizhi gaige shinian*) (Beijing: Economic Management Press and Reform Press), pp. 138–51.

Liu Moshan (1989) 'Primary Consideration for Promoting the CRS' (*tuixing chengbaozhi de chubu fansi*), in *Enterprise Management Reference* (*qiye guanli cankao*), 17 August 1989, pp. 14–17.

Liu Shibai (1987) 'On Socialist commercial economic concepts' (*lun shehui zhuyi shangpin jingji yishi*), *Hong Qi*, vol. 1, pp. 23–7.

Liu Yaojin (1989) 'Ten changes of value systems in ten years reform' (*shinian gaige zhong jiazhiguan de shige zhuanbian*), *Workers' Daily*, quoted in *New China's Monthly Report* (*xinhua yubao*), vol. 2, pp. 13–16.

Liu Zishen and Sun Yong (1993) 'Dialogue on problems of the reform and development in 1993' (*1993 nian gaige yu fazhan wenti manhua*), *Shougang Research and Development* (*Shougang yanjiu yu kaifa*), vol. 6, pp. 24–8.

Lockett, M. (1988) 'Culture and the problems of Chinese management', *Organization Studies*, vol. 9, no. 4, pp. 475–96.

Lu, Yuan (1988) 'Organizational Culture, Strategic Choice and Organizational Behaviour in Chinese Enterprises', *Doctoral Working Paper Series* no. 127 (Birmingham: Aston University).

Lu, Yuan (1991) 'A longitudinal study of Chinese managerial behaviour: an inside view of decision making under the economic reform', unpublished PhD thesis (Birmingham: Aston University).

Lu, Yuan and R. Heard (1995) 'Socialized economic action: a comparison of strategic investment decision-making in China and Britain', *Organization Studies*, vol. 16, no. 3, pp. 395–424.

Ma Hong (1979) 'On problems of economic systems reform' (*guanyu jingji tizhi gaige wenti*), in Ma Hong (ed.) *Economic structure and economic management* (*jingji jiegou yu jingji guanli*) (Beijing: The People's Press, 1982), pp. 125–47.

Ma Hong and Sun Shangqing (eds) (1994) *Economic situation and prospect of China* (*zhongguo jingji xingshi yu zhanwang*) (Beijing: China Development Press).

Ma Quanshan (1989) 'Chinese tradition and Chinese enterprise management', in Jiang Yiwei and Min Jianshu (eds), *Ancient management thoughts and Chinese management* (*gudai guanli sixiang yu Zhongguo shi guanli*) (Beijing: Economic Management Press), pp. 167–76.

MacMurray, Trevor and Jonathan Woetzel (1994) 'The challenge facing China's state-owned enterprises', *The McKinsey Quarterly*, vol. 2, pp. 61–74.

March, James G. (1981) 'Footnotes to organizational change', *Administrative Science Quarterly*, vol 26, pp. 563–77.

Marsh, Paul, Patrick Barwise, Kathryn Thomas and Robin Wensley (1988) 'Managing strategic investment decisions', in Andrew Pettigrew (ed.), *Competitive and management process* (Oxford: Basil Blackwell), pp. 86–136.

Maxwell, N. and B. McFarlane (eds) (1984) *China's changed road to development* (Oxford: Pergamon).

Meyer, J. and B. Rowan (1977) 'Institutionalized organizations: formal structure as myth and ceremony', *American Journal of Sociology*, vol. 83, no. 2, pp. 340–63.

Ministry of Finance (1988) 'Reforming fiscal treasury and tax system' (*caizheng shuishou tizhi de gaige*), in SCRES (ed.), *Ten years of China's economic systems reform* (*zhongguo jingji tizhi gaige shi nian*) (Beijing: Economic Management Press and Reform Press), pp. 493–502.

Mintzberg, Henry (1979) *The structuring of organizations* (Englewood Cliffs, NJ: Prentice-Hall).

Mintzberg, Henry, Duru Raisinghani and André Theoret (1976) 'The structure of "unstructured" decision processes', *Administrative Science Quarterly*, vol. 21, pp. 246–75.

Modern Enterprise Institutional Investigation Team (1993) 'Establishing a modern enterprise institution suitable to the socialist market economy' (*jianli yu shehui zhuyi shichang jingji tizhi xiang shiying de xiandai qiye zhidu*), *People's Daily*, 21 December 1993, quoted in *New China Digest* (*xinhua wenzhai*), vol. 1 (1994), pp. 46–9.

Montias, John M. (1988) 'On hierarchies and economic reforms', *Journal of Institutional and Theoretical Economics*, vol. 144, pp. 832–8.

Mun Kin-Chok (1985) 'An integration of the socialist market and planning in China', in *Marketing Investment, and Management in China and Hong Kong* (Hong Kong: Kwang Jing), pp. 207–19.

Myers, Howard (1982) 'Hidden Goals in Chinese industrialization: Lessons from early modernization attempts', *Columbia Journal of World Business*, vol. 17, no. 4, pp. 74–8.

Nee, Victor (1992) 'Organizational dynamics of market transition', *Administrative Science Quarterly*, vol. 37, pp. 1–27.

Oksenberg, Michel (1974) 'Methods of communication within the Chinese bureaucracy', *China Quarterly*, vol. 57, pp. 1–39.

Olve, Nils-Goran (1986) 'Teaching managers in China: some impressions and reflections', *Management Education and Development*, vol. 17, no. 3, pp. 236–42.

People's Daily, 20 June 1988, p. 2, 'The urgent point is to strengthen management in enterprises' (*dangwu zhiji shi jiaqiang qiye guanlil*).

People's Daily (overseas edition), 31 December 1994, p. 1, '1994's total domestic production values exceeding 4000 billion Yuan' (*1994 guonei shengchan zongzhi tupuo siwanyi daguan*).

People's Daily (overseas edition), 8 February 1995, p. 1, 'The State Economic and Trade Commission announced the key issues relating to the reform of state enterprises in this year' (*guojia jingmao wei gongbu guoyou qiye jinnian gaige yaodian*).

People's University (1980) *Chinese socialist industrial enterprise management (zhongguo shehui zhuyi gongye qiye guanli)* (Beijing: The People's University Press).

Pettigrew, Andrew (1973) *Politics of organizational decision making* (London: Tavistock).

Pettigrew, Andrew (1985a) *An awakening giant: continuity and change in ICI* (Oxford: Basil Blackwell).

Pettigrew, Andrew (1985b) 'Examining change in the long-term context of culture and politics', in Johannes M. Pennings *et al., Organizational strategy and change* (London: Jossey-Bass), pp. 269–318.

Pettigrew, Andrew (ed.) (1988) *The management of strategic change* (Oxford: Basil Blackwell).

Pettigrew, Andrew (1989) 'Longitudinal field research on change: theory and practice', in R. M. Mansfield (ed.), *Frontiers of management* (London: Routledge), pp. 21–49.

Pye, L. W. (1985) *Asian Power and Politics* (Cambridge, Mass.: Harvard University Press).

Redding, S. Gordon and Michael Ng (1982) 'The role of "face" in the organizational perceptions of Chinese managers', *Organization Studies*, vol. 3, no. 3, pp. 201–19.

Reekie, W. D., D. E. Allen and J. N. Crook (1991) *The economics of modern business*, 2nd edn (Oxford: Blackwell).

Ren Tao, Sun Huaiyang and Liu Jinglin (1980) 'The performance of experiment of expanding enterprise autonomy in Sichuan' *(Sichuan sheng kuoda qiye zizhuquan shidian de chengxiao)*, in *Collection of Economic Essays 1980 (jingji xue wenji 1980)* (Hangzhou: Zhejiang People's Press), pp. 422–36.

Riskin, Carl (1987) *China's Political Economy* (Oxford: Oxford University Press).

Schurmann, Franz (1966) *Ideology and organization in communist China* (Berkeley: University of California Press).

Shenkar, Oded and Simcha Ronan (1987) 'Structure and importance of work goals among managers in the People's Republic of China', *Academy of Management Journal*, vol. 30, pp. 564–76.

Simon, Herbert (1976) *Administrative behaviour*, 3rd edn (New York: The Free Press).

Smith, Chris and Paul Thompson (eds) (1992) *Labour in transition: the labour process in Eastern Europe and China* (London: Routledge).

Solinger, D. J. (1989) 'Urban reform and relational contracting in post-Mao China: An interpretation of the transition from plan to market', *Studies in Comparative Communism*, vol. 23, pp. 171–85.

Song Maoguang (1993) 'The evolutionary process of understanding the market' *(dui shichang kanfa de yanjin guocheng)*, *Study of Treasure and Financial Problems (caijing wenti yanjiu)*, no. 11, quoted in *New China Digest (xin hua wen zhai)*, vol. (1994), pp. 49–51.

Spulber, Nicolas (1979) *Organizational alternatives in Soviet-type economies* (Cambridge: Cambridge University Press).

State Council's Finance and Economic System Reform Office (1979) 'Provisional opinion on the general programme of economic administration system reform' *(guanyu jingji tizhi guanli tizhi zongti shexiang de chubu yijian)*, in SCRES (ed.) (1988), *Ten years of China's economic systems reform* (*zhongguo jingji tizhi gaige shinian*) (Beijing: Economic Management Press and Reform Press), pp. 826–34.

'Summary of opinions on the CRS' (1988) (*guanyu chengbao jingying zerenzhi wenti de guandian zongshu*), in *China Industry Research* (*Zhongguo gongye yanjiu*), vol. 3, pp. 77–81.

Sun Jian (1992) *The economic history of the People's Republic of China* (*zhonghua renmin gonghe guo jingji shi*) (Beijing: The People's University Press).

Sun Yefang (1980) 'The internal and external reasons for the law of values' (*jiazhi guilu de neiyin lun he waiyinlun*), in *Collection of Economic Essays 1980* (*jingji xue wenji 1980*) (Hangzhou: Zhejiang People's Press), pp. 1–23.

The Voice of Productive Forces (*shengchan li zhisheng*), vol. 12 (1993), pp. 9–13. 'The unpredictable future of the monetary supply for state enterprises' (*guoyou qiye qianjing moce*).

Thompson, Paul and Chris Smith (1992) 'Socialism and the labour process in theory and practice', in Chris Smith and Paul Thompson (eds), *Labour in transition: the labour process in Eastern Europe and China* (London: Routledge), pp. 3–33.

Tian Yuan, Qiao Gang and Ma Jiantang (1989) 'Policy Suggestion on Rectifying of Inflation in next three years' (*jinhou zhili tonghuo pengzhang de zhengce jianyi*), *Study Materials for Economists* (*jingji gongzuo zhe xuexi cailiao*), vol. 26, pp. 16–25.

Tian Yuan and Qiao Gang (eds) (1991) *Study of China's price reform from 1984 to 1990* (*zhongguo jiage gaige yanjiu: 1984–1990*) (Beijing: Electronic Industry Press).

Tisdell, Clement (1993) *Economic development in the context of China* (London: St. Martin's Press).

Torrington, Derek and Laura Hall (1987) *Personnel management* (New York: Prentice Hall).

Walder, Andrew (1986) *Communist neo-traditionalism: work and authority in Chinese industry* (Berkeley: University California Press).

Walder, Andrew (1987) 'Wage reform and the web of factory interests', *China Quarterly*, no. 109, pp. 22–41.

Walder, Andrew (1989) 'Factory and manager in an era of reform', *China Quarterly*, no. 118, pp. 242–64.

Wang Aiwen (1991) 'Reform of our country's labour planning administrative systems' (*woguo laodong jihua guanli tizhi gaige*), in Xia Jizhi and Dang Xiaojie (eds) (1991), *Employment and unemployment in China* (*zhongguo de jiuye yu shiye*) (Beijing: China Labour Press), pp. 240–60.

Wang Dayong (1989) 'Pricing Reform with Inflation' (*zai tonghuo pengzhang de tiaojian xia tuijin jiage gaige*), *China: Development & Reform*, vol. 1, pp. 12–20.

Warner, Malcolm (1986) 'The "Long March" of Chinese management education, 1979–84', *China Quarterly*, no. 106, pp. 326–42.

Warner, Malcolm (1992) *How Chinese managers learn* (London: Macmillan).

Wei Zhengtong (1988) *Breakthrough of ethical principles* (*lunli sixiang de tupuo*) (Chengdu: Sichuan People's Press).

Wen Guifang (1989) 'Review and Prospect of Pricing Adjustment and Reform in Our Country' (*woguo jiage tiaozheng he gaige de huigu yu qianzhan*), *Study Materials for Economists* (*jingji gongzuozhe xuexi ziliao*), vol. 34 (1989), pp. 15–50.

Whipp, Richard, Robert Rosenfeld and Andrew Pettigrew (1988) 'Understanding strategic change processes', in Andrew Pettigrew (ed.), *The management of strategic change* (Oxford: Basil Blackwell), pp. 14–55.

Wilczynski, J. (1972) *Socialist economic development and reforms* (London: Macmillan).

World Bank (1985) *China: long term development issues and options* (Baltimore and London: The Johns Hopkins University Press).

World Bank (1988) *China: finance and investment* (Washington: The World Bank Press).

Wu Jinglian (1988) 'Preface', in Wu Jinglian and Zhou Xiaochuan (eds), *The integrated design of China's economic reform* (Beijing: China Outlook Press).

Wu Jinglian (1989) 'Evolution of economic theories and choice of reform strategy: analysis of China's practice' (*jingji lilun de yanbian yu gaige zhanlue de xuanze: dui zhongguo shili de fenxi*), *Study and Practice* (*xuexi yu shijian*), vol. 6, pp. 3–10.

Wu Jinglian (1992) *A road to a market economy* (*tongxiang shichang jingji zhilu*) (Beijing: Beijing Industrial Polytechnic University Press).

Wu Jinglian (1993) *Planned Economy or Market Economy* (*jihua jingji haishi shichap jingji*) (Beijing: China Economic Press).

Wu Jinglian, Liu Jirui, Li Jiange and Zhang Junkuo (1986) 'Modernization needs entrepreneurs and entrepreneurs need reform' (*xiandaihua xuyao de qiyejia yu qiyejia xuyao de gaige*), in Wu Jinglian and Zhou Xiaochuang (eds), *The integrated design of China's economic reform* (Beijing: China Outlook Press, 1988), pp. 278–87.

Wu Zhenkun and Chen Wentong (eds) (1993) *Overview of China's economic systems reform* (*zhongguo jingji tizhi gaige tonglun*) (Beijing: Beijing Industrial Polytechnic University Press).

Xia Jizhi and Dang Xiaojie (eds) (1991) *Employment and unemployment in China* (*zhongguo de jiuye yu shiye*) (Beijing: China Labour Press).

Xie Youqiao and Wang Dong (eds) (1992) *Theory, policy and experiences* (*lilun zhengce jingyan*) (Changchun: Jilin People's Press).

Xu Dixin (1982) *The change in China's national economy* (*zhonguo guomin jingji de biange*) (Beijing: Social Science Press).

Xu Feiqing and Wang Shengrui (eds) (1993) *China's economic systems reform* (*zhongguo de jingji tizhi gaige*) (Beijing: China Finance and Economic Press).

Yuan Baohua (1989a) 'Change and Development in Enterprise Management in Ten Years of reform' (*shinian gaige zhong woguo qiye guanli de bianhua yu fazhan*) speech at the tenth anniversary of China's Enterprise Management Association, 3 March, 1989, Beijing.

Yuan Baohua (1989b) 'A speech in the Economic Committee of the National Political Consultative Conference', *Chinese Enterprise Newspaper* (*zhongguo qiye bao*), 6 February, pp. 1–3.

Zhang Pan and Zhang Wenzhong (1989) 'Three investigation reports' (*san xiang diaocha baogao*). *Study Materials for Economists* (*jingji gongzuo zhe xuexi cailiao*), no. 34, pp. 8–15.

Zhang Shaojie, Cui Hening, Zu Gang and Ji Xiaoming (1987), 'Investment: initial changes in the mechanism and preliminary idea about the reform', in B. L. Reynolds (ed.), *Reform in China: challenges & choices* (New York: M. E. Sharpe), pp. 108–29.

Zhang Xiaojian, Yu Faming, Mao Jian, Dang Xiaojie and Mo Rong (1991) 'Problems in our country's labour development strategy' (*woguo laodong jiuye de fazhan zhanlue wenti*), in Xia Jizhi and Dang Xiaojie (eds), *Employment and unemployment in China* (*zhongguo de jiuye yu shiye*) (Beijing: China Labour Press), pp. 23–59.

Zhang Zhenhuan (1987) 'Contractual business enterprises urgently need a new relationship between the party and administration' (*chengbao qiye jixuqueli xinxing dangzheng guanxi*), *Hebei Daily*, 7 October, 1987, p. 4.

Zhang Zuoyuan (1988) 'Review of the price reform in the past 10 years and its prospects' (*shinian jiage gaige de huigu yu qianzhan*), in SCRES (ed.), *Ten years of China's economic systems reform* (*zhongguo jingji tizhi gaige shinian*) (Beijing: Economic Management Press and Reform Press), pp. 420–8.

Zhao Lukuan and Lu Guotai (1992) 'Employment and wages in cities and towns', in George Totten and Zhou Shulian (eds), *China's economic reform* (Oxford: Westview Press), pp. 181–96.

Zhao Ziyang (1986) 'Report on the *Seventh Five-Year Plan*' quoted in SCRES (ed.), (1988), *Ten years of China's economic systems reform* (*zhongguo jingji tizhi gaige shinian*) (Beijing: Economic Management Press and Reform Press), pp. 83–7.

Zhao Ziyang (1987) 'Speech at the 13th National Congress of the Party', October 1987, quoted in SCRES (ed.), *Ten years of China's economic systems reform* (*zhongguo jingji tizhi gaige shinian*) (Beijing: Economic Management Press and Reform Press), pp. 90–8.

Zhao Ziyang (1988) speech at the 3rd plenary session of the Central Party Committee (*zai zhongguo gongchandang shishanjie sanzhong quanhuishang de baogao*), *Economic Daily*, 28 October, 1988, pp. 1–2.

Zheng Xuemeng, Jian Zhaocheng and Zhang Wenyi (1984) *Short History of the Chinese Economy* (*jianming zhongguo jingji tongshi*) (Harbin: Heilongjiang People's Press).

Zhong Chengxun (ed.) (1993) *Study of local government investment behaviour* (*di fang zhengfu tou zi xing wei*) (Beijing: China Treasure Press).

Zhou Enlai (1975) 'Towards the Great Goal of the Four Modernizations' (*xiang sige siandaihua de hongwei mubiao qianjin*), *People's Daily*, 21 January 1975.

Zhou Shulian (1992) 'Enterprise vitality and macro-management', in George Totten and Zhou Shulian (eds), *China's economic reform* (Oxford: Westview Press), pp. 99–123.

Zhu Jiaming and Lu Zheng (1984) *Reality and choice: contemporary China's industrial structures and institutions* (*xianshi yu xuanze, dangdai zhongguo gongye jiegou yu tizhi*) (Chengdu: Sichuan People's Press).

Zhu Min (1988) 'Review of prices in our country in 1987' (*1987 woguo wujia gaishu*), *Practice and Theory of Price* (*jiage lilun yu shijian*), no. 6, pp. 2–10.

Zhu Rongji (1986) 'What China wants now from foreigners', *International Management*, April, pp. 54–5.

Zi Zhongyun (1987) 'The relationship of Chinese traditional culture to the modernization of China', *Asian Survey*, vol. 27, no. 4, pp. 442–58.

Zou Xiangqun (1993) 'Price policies in the establishment of a socialist-market economic system' (*jianli shehui zhuyi shichang jingji tizhi zhong de jiage duice*), in China Central Party University (ed.), *Authoritative people talking about the transformation from a planned economy to a market one* (*quanwei renshi tan cong jihua jingji zhuanxiang shichang jingji*) (Beijing: China Central Party University Press), pp. 151–8.

Index